PRAISE FOR
HOW FASCISM WORKS

"A vital read for a nation under Trump . . . [An] arresting new book . . . The book provides a fascinating breakdown of the fascist ideology. . . . Stanley includes smaller observations that may for some readers land bracingly close to home." —*The Guardian*

"By placing Trump in transnational and transhistorical perspective, Stanley sees patterns that others miss. . . . Stanley's comparative perspective is particularly effective in illustrating how fascists use fears of sexual violence."
—*The New York Times Book Review* (Editors' Choice)

"[A] brilliantly written study on the revival of fascism . . . It comes at the right time." —*Die Zeit*

"Remarkable . . . An important book . . . Books like these . . . are welcome: they help to thin out the returning darkness, harbingers, as you know, of monsters."
—*Corriere Della Sera*

"Should appeal to anyone who cares for democracy and human dignity." —*Frontline*

"Jason Stanley reveals how the liberties of the people wither when voters embrace politicians who promote the divisive politics of Us versus Them, while denigrating cooperation, compromise, and respect for others. *How Fascism Works* builds on philosopher Stanley's insightful *How Propaganda Works* to explain in concise and easily understood terms how people get tricked into reversing the expanding rights that made America great."

—DAVID CAY JOHNSTON, Pulitzer Prize winner and author of *It's Even Worse Than You Think: What the Trump Administration Is Doing to America* and *The Making of Donald Trump*

"A sharply argued and timely guide to the stories and tactics used by right-wing movements and regimes from the 1920s to the present day. Stanley's highlighting of the politics of sexual anxiety is particularly welcome and relevant."

—RUTH BEN-GHIAT, author of *Italian Fascism's Empire Cinema*

"There are moments in which the fate of humanity itself hangs in the balance, and such times always bring with them the resurrection of ugly myths. And yet, as Jason Stanley, one of this nation's most important philosophers, makes clear, when such myths are deconstructed and their history is laid bare, we remember the extraordinary ties that in fact bind us together. And, in the fire of that powerful recollection, modern-day fascism—the current myth-dependent moment of intolerance, xenophobia, and fearmongering that we find ourselves in—can be rendered to ash."

—HEATHER ANN THOMPSON, Pulitzer Prize–winning author of *Blood in the Water: The Attica Prison Uprising of 1971 and Its Legacy*

"Jason Stanley's book comes at a most propitious time when we must come to grips with the political consequences that may follow xenophobic populism currently on the rise in the western world. History teaches what those consequences are, and in his book Stanley, with great analytical and conceptual clarity, not only tells the story but more crucially provides a critical framework through which to see the insidious mechanisms at play that are threatening today's democracies around the globe. *How Fascism Works* is a must-read for all of us who take seriously our responsibility as citizens."

—JAN T. GROSS, emeritus professor of history at Princeton University, author of *Neighbors: The Destruction of the Jewish Community in Jedwabne, Poland* and *Fear: Anti-Semitism in Poland After Auschwitz*

"A potent call for democracies to resist the insidious encroachment of fascism." —*Kirkus Reviews*

BY JASON STANLEY

How Fascism Works: The Politics of Us and Them

How Propaganda Works

Know How

Knowledge and Practical Interests

Language in Context

HOW FASCISM WORKS

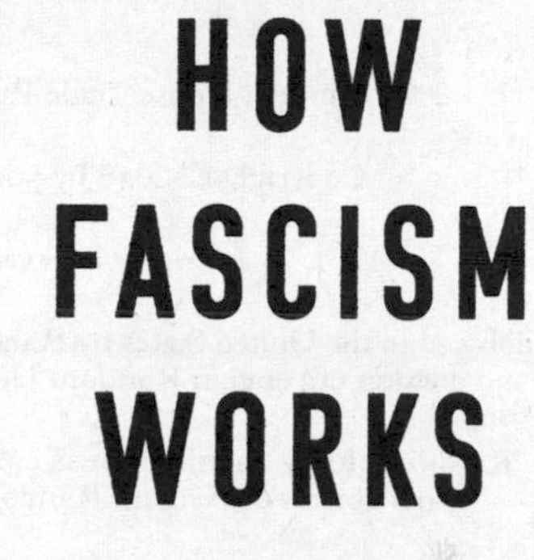

HOW FASCISM WORKS

THE POLITICS OF US AND THEM

JASON STANLEY

RANDOM HOUSE TRADE PAPERBACK
NEW YORK

2020 Random House Trade Paperback Edition

Published in the United States by Random House, an imprint and division of Penguin Random House LLC, New York.

Random House and the House colophon are registered trademarks of Penguin Random House LLC.

Originally published in hardcover in the United States by Random House, an imprint and division of Penguin Random House LLC, in 2018.

Library of Congress Cataloging-in-Publication Data
Names: Stanley, Jason, author.
Title: How fascism works: the politics of us and them / Jason Stanley.
Description: First edition. | New York: Random House, [2018]
Includes bibliographical references and index.
Identifiers: LCC 2018013266 | ISBN 978-0-525-51185-4 [TP]
ISBN 978-0-525-51184-7 (ebook)
Subjects: LCSH: Fascism. | Polarization (Social sciences)—Political aspects.
Classification: LCC JC481 .S67 2018 | DDC 321.9/4—dc23
LC record available at https://lccn.loc.gov/20180113266

Printed in the United States of America on acid-free paper

randomhousebooks.com

9

Title page image by Everett Historical/Shutterstock.com

Book design by Jo Anne Metsch

To Emile, Alain, Kalev, Talia,
and their generation

PREFACE TO THE PAPERBACK EDITION

Since publishing *How Fascism Works* in September 2018, global events have only substantiated my concerns about modern fascism. The political leaders, parties, and movements I wrote about then have made advances on their agendas. New leaders and political parties have emerged emulating the tactics I describe. The coronavirus, declared a pandemic by the WHO on March 11, 2020, has threatened fundamental aspects of human, social, and political life and led to a global economic crisis. Understanding the lessons of this book has acquired an urgency even I did not predict.

I wrote this book as a warning about fascist politics, essentially the danger of rhetoric that encourages fear and anger as a means to foment ethnic and religious division, seeping into public discourse. Today, the effects of such talk seem clear, as that rhetoric now shapes the outcome of elections and makes its way into policies.

Jair Bolsonaro, "the tropical Trump," was not mentioned in the original edition of this book. Yet soon after it was published, he was elected president of Brazil, the world's fourth-largest democracy. Bolsonaro ran an anti-corruption campaign centered on the theme of Law and Order. He was openly anti-feminist and anti-gay, and he repeatedly lauded the country's past of military dictatorship. Since he has been in office, "[a]ll three of Bolsonaro's politically active sons, along with his wife Michelle, have been implicated in corruption scandals."[1] In Brazil right now, journalists are being threatened. Universities, a source of protest against Bolsonaro, as well as a target of his political demagoguery, face huge cuts in research funding. On March 15, 2020, far-right-wing demonstrations were held across the country, calling to disband Congress and the courts. Bolsonaro, like Trump, is a climate change denier. Brazil's Amazon rainforest, whose health is crucial for that of the planet, has faced increasingly catastrophic fires under Bolsonaro's watch and concomitant increased deforestation.

For years in Europe, there was talk of a "Spanish exception" to the rise of the far right in Europe; supposedly their long experience of fascism in the twentieth century protected them from making the same mistake again. In 2018, this ended, as Vox, a far-right party harkening back to Spain's fascist dictator Franco, raising fear and panic

[1] https://www.theguardian.com/commentisfree/2019/oct/28/jair-bolsonaro-brazil-paramilitaries-corruption-david-miranda.

about immigration and loss of traditional culture, was formed. In 2019, Vox became Spain's third largest political party in Parliament, following the country's elections.

People often assume that fascist tactics can achieve success only where democratic institutions, and commitment to democratic culture, is already weak. We are thus told to pay attention to policies and institutions rather than the rhetoric they can follow. But Sweden is a country with some of the world's most stable democratic institutions. It has first-rate public goods—excellent universal health care, education, and day care. The commitment of individual Swedes to democratic values has rarely been questioned. It is a disturbing sign of the power of fascist tactics that the only Swedish political party that characteristically employs them, the Sweden Democrats, has as of this writing become the most popular Swedish political party. The neo-fascist party AfD is the third-strongest party in Germany, another country whose democratic institutions have been beyond question. Across the world, politicians and political parties have learned from the examples discussed here, about how rhetoric of ethnic and racial division can go on to win elections and popular support.

Since the book was published, there have not just been new developments—there have also been worrisome advances in existing movements. Panic about immigration and the fear of losing the dominant culture to religious or ethnic minorities loathed by the majority groups are central to fascist politics. In the countries in which these tactics are most successful, we now see the clear emergence of fascist policies. India is a key example in this book, particularly the rise of the Hindu nationalist Bharatiya Janata Party (BJP) and its leader, Narendra Modi. Since this book was written, BJP has won a majority in India and has moved to implement disturbing policies.

India's citizenship practices since its founding have been liberal and secular. But under the control of BJP, the country is dramatically transforming. India has a National Population Registry and a Census. But both of these count residents, not citizens. In November 2019, India's Parliament proposed to add a National Register of Citizens (NRC). The task of the NRC is to make decisions about who is and who is not a citizen, to divide the citizens from the non-citizens. Those deemed to be non-citizens will be scheduled for detention and eventual deportation. India has a large body of residents born in India but lacking documentation such as birth certificates that establish this fact. Decisions must be made about who among them should count as a citizen and who should not. There is significant concern, legitimated by the parties behind this project, that the decision will be made on the basis of religion: Muslim residents without the right paperwork will be subject to detention and deportation; Hindus without the right paperwork will be added to the registry.

At the same time that the NRC is devising criteria for

which undocumented residents will count as citizens, India has passed the Citizenship Amendment Bill (CAB). CAB promises a fast path to citizenship for immigrants belonging to specified religious groups. Muslims who cannot prove their citizenship are excluded from a path to citizenship in the CAB guidelines; Hindus who cannot prove their citizenship have one. In India, we are witnessing a transition from liberal citizenship practices to fascist ones. BJP's fascist politics are not merely rhetorical.

A distinguishing mark of fascist politics is the targeting of ideological enemies and the freeing of all restraints in combating them. In India, Brazil, and the United States—and everywhere else where such politics has seized the imagination—universities have been one of the main focal points of attack by far-right party leaders. In January 2020, Jawaharlal Nehru University in New Delhi was attacked by Hindu nationalists. While police stood by, they rampaged through the university, beating students and professors alike. Commenting in *The Indian Express* on the shocking violence, clearly green-lit by the government, Pratap Mehta wrote:

> The targeting of enemies—minorities, liberals, secularists, leftists, urban naxals, intellectuals, assorted protestors—is not driven by a calculus of ordinary politics. . . . When you legitimize yourself entirely by inventing enemies, the truth ceases to matter, normal restraints of

> civilization and decency cease to matter, the checks and balances of normal politics cease to matter.[2]

Turning to the United States, I began this project alarmed by the success of the fascist political tactics Donald Trump employed in his 2015 candidacy announcement. What does the course of subsequent political events reveal? Was Trump's harsh rhetoric against Mexican immigrants and Muslims mere political tactics? Or in the intervening years, have there been changes in institutions and policies in clearly fascist directions, as in the case of BJP and India?

On January 27, 2017, the Trump Administration issued one of its first executive orders, with the title *Protecting the Nation from Foreign Terrorist Entry into the United States*. It halted indefinitely the admission of refugees from the war in Syria, and placed a ban on travel into the United States by citizens of seven Muslim majority countries. It was ultimately superseded by two replacement travel prohibitions, trying to overcome obvious legal objections because banning based on religious identity is manifestly inconsistent with the Establishment Clause of the U.S. Constitution. The third version of the legislation was adjusted to include two non-Muslim majority countries, North Korea and Venezuela, on its list of "Countries of Identified Concern," whose nationals the order

[2] Pratab Bhanu Mehta, "JNU violence reflects an apocalyptical politics driven by a constant need to find new enemies," *The Indian Express*, January 7, 2020.

bans from entry to the United States. The Supreme Court ruled, in a 5–4 decision, that this adjustment made the executive order consistent with the Establishment Clause (despite obviously being crafted for just this purpose). In the ensuing years, this ban on many of the world's Muslims from entry to the United States has become normalized. It is no longer a salient topic of discussion in the U.S. media. Trump's fascist political tactics quickly were made material in policies of explicit exclusion.

In the epilogue of this book, I speculated about the other sites where Trump's fascist political tactics would most likely first take material form:

> In the United States, as Donald Trump's campaign against immigration intensifies, it is sweeping untold numbers of undocumented workers of all backgrounds into anonymously run private detention centers, where they are concealed from view and public concern.

This continues to happen. At the U.S./Mexico border, the United States has established detention centers where undocumented migrants are held as they await legal hearings. Family separation has been a key, cruel feature of these sites. In June 2019, Representative Alexandria Ocasio-Cortez created a furor by describing these private detention camps as "concentration camps." But Ocasio-Cortez's description is accurate. Like concentration camps in Germany in the 1930s, they are hidden from public view. Journalists are barred from visiting these centers; they are open only to legal representatives and members of Congress.[3] In early June, the Trump administration canceled educational, recreational, and legal aid for migrant children in detention centers, sealing them off further from public scrutiny. Reports of the extreme conditions in these centers have flooded the news. These reports have been provided by legal representatives empowered to visit them. What happens now that official funding is cut off for such visits?

Even as we are shut off from facts, immigrants will hear the stories from one another. The strategy here is to encourage them to self-deport. This, too, is familiar from history. In the November 1938 pogrom of German Jews, more than 30,000 of them were rounded up and sent to concentration camps, where they were subjected to brutal and inhumane conditions and soon released. Nikolaus Wachsmann, a professor of European history at the University of London, explains that the release of these prisoners made sense from the regime's perspective, because "the camps had served their function—forcing many Jews out of Germany."[4] The regime's harsh anti-Semitic rhetoric, followed by exposure of its Jewish citizens to the brutality of its camps, led to a large exodus of Jews from Germany

[3] I am grateful to Kica Matos of the Vera Institute of Justice for educating me about the situation.

[4] Nikolaus Wachsmann, *KL: A History of Concentration Camps* (New York: Farrar, Straus and Giroux, 2015), 186.

(including my grandmother and my father in July 1939). The tactic worked. Should we therefore employ it?

There is an economic reality to this situation as well. We increasingly see connections between powerful business interests and the institutions of state terror. Wall Street gives billions in loans to facilitate the profits of companies who run detention centers; large companies make profits by selling their wares to them, and former high-ranking administration officials serve on their boards. On the local level, county jails bolster their budgets by housing those detained by ICE's massively broadened mandate. The legal, material, and economic structure of these camps is evocative of Nazi Germany's early concentration camps.

There are also arguably institutions in the United States, not created by Trump, but certainly adopted and radically empowered by his administration, that resemble fascist paramilitary organizations. ICE is a novel American institution—it was created in 2003 by the Homeland Security Act in the wake of September 11, at a time when rights and liberties took a back seat to concerns about safety. The same act created the Bureau of Customs and Border Protection, tasked with policing the border and staffing migrant detention centers. In ICE, we have a special force, created in an anti-democratic moment in American history, authorized with police-like power and directed at political outsiders inside our borders. The institution itself is tied politically to the country's leader. Trump is the first president endorsed by a major union representing ICE's employees, and Trump has repeatedly called himself its chief defender.

ICE is an organization that is like the police but is not the police. The job of the police in a democratic society is to keep communities safe. In practice, ICE collaborates with conventional American criminal justice institutions, including local police departments, but often ends up working at cross-purposes with them by creating fear in immigrant communities, whose members become less likely to report crime. As a result, some police chiefs have aligned themselves against ICE raids. The goal of ICE is not to make communities safer. ICE's mission is to reinforce a distinction between "us" and "them."

When observing the tangible effects of Trump's rhetoric, many in the media look to the streets for hate crimes by skinheads, or for other examples of extrajudicial violence aimed at Trump's targets—immigrants and Muslims, for example—but not actually committed by the Trump administration. This is dangerously confused. It is a reaction that masks the worst material effects of Trump's political tactics. Fascist political tactics employed by an election's winner materialize in the resulting state apparatus, not only between individuals. Debates that require one to direct one's eye instead to the streets force us to look away from the structural consequences of fascist rhetoric. By ignoring the state apparatus erected by those who entered into office through fascist politics, we behave as if fascist political tactics cannot transform once-democratic states into fascist ones. This is a thesis that history, as well as common sense, rejects.

In German history, the term "Gleichschaltung" connotes the process by which the institutions of the German government gradually became "Nazified," moving from liberal democratic organizing principles to National Socialist ones, principally fealty to the Nazi leader, Adolf Hitler. Without comparing the new brand of far-right leaders to Hitler, it is nevertheless possible to see similar processes at work in three of the world's largest democracies—India, the United States, and Brazil. In all three countries, there is movement toward unifying institutions around loyalty to an ethnic identity, as in India, or loyalty to a single leader, as in the United States, where the most powerful political party is increasingly defined by fealty to Donald Trump. This threatens the democratic nature of these institutions as well as their competence to carry out their institutional missions. Our democratic culture is on life support.

Behind this transnational ultranationalist movement are the forces of capital. Tech giants and media benefit from the dramatic clash of friend and enemy. Fear and anger get people to the polls, but they also keep people online and glued to the media. Oil companies benefit when ultranationalist movements represent international climate change agreements, such as the Paris Agreement, as threats to national sovereignty. The weaker individual states and international agreements are, the stronger the power of multinational corporations becomes.

India, the United States, and Brazil are now run by far-right parties, with demagogic leaders implementing ultranationalist agendas. In the bastions of democracy in Western Europe, far-right parties are ascendant. All around the world, liberal democracy is in retreat. Not since the middle of the twentieth century has liberal democracy been in such peril.

With the advent of a public health pandemic like COVID-19, the attacks on expertise, science, and truth that are the lifeblood of fascist politics imperil much more than just our political system. We can see the explicit dangers in the response to COVID-19 of the leaders of the United States, Brazil, and India, which was initially to dismiss the virus as an overblown hoax.[5] The response of these governments to the virus was not some accident—as I show in the pages to follow, fascist ideology conflicts *in principle* with expertise, science, and truth.

Fascist politics exploits crises to advance its ideological agenda. Trump called the virus "the Chinese virus" in part because that is where it originated. But the reason he sticks to this label in the face of criticism is to reframe debate around nationalist conflict (and away from the incompetence of his administration). And when it began to take the virus seriously, the Trump administration immediately sought to use it as a means to justify retroactively its nationalist agenda of closing borders, and its suspicion

[5] https://www.theguardian.com/world/2020/mar/22/brazilians-protest-bolsonaro-coronavirus-panelaco.

of immigrants, by associating immigrants (and "sanctuary cities") with the virus. As I show in this book, fascism in power seeks to make its rhetoric into reality—for example, by immiserating and impoverishing populations it represents as diseased. In early March, Trump's Executive Office for Immigration Review ordered immigration court staff "to remove CDC posters designed to slow spread of coronavirus."[6] It's hard to see what the point of such an order is, except to give some reality to the association between immigrants and the virus by failing to inform these populations of the dangers.

The Hungarian government's response to the virus has been to introduce legislation to disband Parliament and let Victor Orbán rule by emergency decree. In the United States, the Department of Justice sought emergency powers from Congress, including indefinite detention by judges. Using crisis as anti-democratic opportunity is a classic fascist tactic.

If one looks on the international level, the situation may appear hopeless. However, this book suggests a different reaction. A moral of this book is that fascism is not a new threat, but rather a permanent temptation. The United States has captured the attention of the world not because of its fascist history, but because of the heroism its residents have exhibited in internal fights against it. From the Civil War to the Civil Rights Movement, the United

[6] https://nymag.com/intelligencer/2020/03/what-was-trump-dojs-problem-with-covid-prevention-posters.html.

States has fought against white Christian nationalism, no less than Europe has fought against its own ultranationalist movements. Brazil threw off its military dictatorship; India was founded on secular liberal principles, with a clear-eyed view of the dangers of the very religious nationalism it now faces (yet again).

We must also remember that the structures that preserve our democracies against the current threats have long been in place. In each of our local communities, there is at least one activist who has been dealing with a problem for generations. It was under Obama that the current harsh deportation regime started in the United States. In my community of New Haven, Kica Matos was the director of immigrant rights and racial justice at the Center for Community Change, where she coordinated the nation's largest network of immigrant rights organizations. During the Trump era, she has redoubled her efforts, joining the city of New Haven as an advisor and the Vera Institute of Justice as the director of the Center for Immigration and Justice. The wisdom and courage of lifelong activists such as Matos informs this book—through democratic activists throughout our communities, we can be reminded that the struggles we face are ongoing, and the forces—on both sides—strong.

It remains for us to join that struggle, realizing that it's not to overcome a moment, but rather to make a permanent democratic commitment.

CONTENTS

INTRODUCTION

Growing up with parents who'd fled Europe as refugees, I was raised with stories of the heroic nation that helped defeat Hitler's armies and usher in an unprecedented era of liberal democracy in the West. Near the end of his life, gravely ill with Parkinson's disease, my father insisted on visiting the beaches of Normandy. Leaning on the shoulder of his wife, my stepmother, he fulfilled a lifelong dream, walking where so many brave American youth lost their lives in the battle against fascism. But even as my family celebrated and honored this American legacy, my parents also knew that American heroism and American ideas of freedom have never been just one thing.

Before World War II, Charles Lindbergh typified American heroism with his daring flights, including the first solo transatlantic flight, and his celebration of new technology. He parlayed his fame and heroic stature into a leading role in the America First movement, which opposed America's entrance into the war against Nazi Germany. In 1939, in an essay entitled "Aviation, Geography, and Race," published in that most American of journals, *Reader's Digest,* Lindbergh embraced something close to Nazism for America:

> It is time to turn from our quarrels and to build our White ramparts again. This alliance with foreign races means nothing but death to us. It is our turn to guard our heritage from Mongol and Persian and Moor, before we become engulfed in a limitless foreign sea.[1]

The year 1939 was also when my father, Manfred, then six years old, escaped Nazi Germany, leaving Tempelhof Airport in Berlin in July with his mother, Ilse, after spending months in hiding. He arrived in New York City on August 3, 1939, his ship sailing past the Statue of Liberty on its way to dock. We have a family album from the 1920s and '30s. The last page has six different pictures of the Statue of Liberty gradually coming into view.

The America First movement was the public face of pro-fascist sentiment in the United States at that time.[2] In the twenties and thirties, many Americans shared Lindbergh's views against immigration, especially by non-Europeans. The Immigration Act of 1924 strictly limited immigration into the country, and it was specifically intended to restrict the immigration of both nonwhites and

Jews. In 1939, the United States allowed so few refugees through its borders that it is a miracle that my father happened to be among them.

In 2016, Donald Trump revived "America First" as one of his slogans, and from his first week in office, his administration has ceaselessly pursued travel bans on immigration, including refugees, specifically singling out Arab countries. Trump also promised to deport the millions of nonwhite Central and South American undocumented workers in the United States and to end legislation protecting the children they brought with them from deportation. In September 2017, the Trump administration set a cap of forty-five thousand on the number of refugees that will be allowed into the United States in 2018, the lowest number since presidents began placing such limits.

If Trump recalled Lindbergh specifically with "America First," the rest of his campaign also longed for some vague point in history—to "Make America Great Again." But when, exactly, was America great, in the eyes of the Trump campaign? During the nineteenth century, when the United States enslaved its black population? During Jim Crow, when black Americans in the South were prevented from voting? A hint about the decade that was most salient to the Trump campaign emerges from a November 18, 2016, *Hollywood Reporter* interview with Steve Bannon, the then president-elect's chief strategist, in which he remarks about the era to come that "it will be as exciting as the 1930s." In short, the era when the United States had its most sympathy for fascism.

. . .

In recent years, multiple countries across the world have been overtaken by a certain kind of far-right nationalism; the list includes Russia, Hungary, Poland, India, Turkey, and the United States. The task of generalizing about such phenomena is always vexing, as the context of each country is always unique. But such generalization is necessary in the current moment. I have chosen the label "fascism" for ultranationalism of some variety (ethnic, religious, cultural), with the nation represented in the person of an authoritarian leader who speaks on its behalf. As Donald Trump declared in his Republican National Convention speech in July 2016, "I am your voice."

My interest in this book is in fascist *politics*. Specifically, my interest is in fascist tactics as a mechanism to achieve power. Once those who employ such tactics come to power, the regimes they enact are in large part determined by particular historical conditions. What occurred in Germany was different from what occurred in Italy. Fascist politics does not necessarily lead to an explicitly fascist state, but it is dangerous nonetheless.

Fascist politics includes many distinct strategies: the mythic past, propaganda, anti-intellectualism, unreality, hierarchy, victimhood, law and order, sexual anxiety, appeals to the heartland, and a dismantling of public welfare and unity. Though a defense of certain elements is legitimate and sometimes warranted, there are times in history when they come together in one party or political movement. These are dangerous moments. In the United States today, Republican politicians employ these strategies with more and more frequency. Their increasing tendency to engage in this politics should give honest conservatives pause.

The dangers of fascist politics come from the particular way in which it dehumanizes segments of the population. By excluding these groups, it limits the capacity for empathy among other citizens, leading to the justification of inhumane treatment, from repression of freedom, mass imprisonment, and expulsion to, in extreme cases, mass extermination.

Genocides and campaigns of ethnic cleansing are regularly preceded by the kinds of political tactics described in this book. In the cases of Nazi Germany, Rwanda, and contemporary Myanmar, the victims of ethnic cleansing were subjected to vicious rhetorical attacks by leaders and in the press for months or years before the regime turned genocidal. With these precedents, it should concern all Americans that as a candidate and as president, Donald Trump has publicly and explicitly insulted immigrant groups.

Fascist politics can dehumanize minority groups even

when an explicitly fascist state does not arise.[3] By some measures, Myanmar is transitioning to a democracy. But five years of brutal rhetoric directed against the Rohingya Muslim population has nevertheless resulted in one of the worst cases of ethnic cleansing since the Second World War.

. . .

The most telling symptom of fascist politics is division. It aims to separate a population into an "us" and a "them." Many kinds of political movements involve such a division; for example, Communist politics weaponizes class divisions. Giving a description of fascist politics involves describing the very specific way that fascist politics distinguishes "us" from "them," appealing to ethnic, religious, or racial distinctions, and using this division to shape ideology and, ultimately, policy. Every mechanism of fascist politics works to create or solidify this distinction.

Fascist politicians justify their ideas by breaking down a common sense of history in creating a **mythic past** to support their vision for the present. They rewrite the population's shared understanding of reality by twisting the language of ideals through **propaganda** and promoting **anti-intellectualism**, attacking universities and educational systems that might challenge their ideas. Eventually, with these techniques, fascist politics creates a state of **unreality**, in which conspiracy theories and fake news replace reasoned debate.

As the common understanding of reality crumbles, fascist politics makes room for dangerous and false beliefs to take root. First, fascist ideology seeks to naturalize group difference, thereby giving the appearance of natural, scientific support for a **hierarchy** of human worth. When social rankings and divisions solidify, fear fills in for understanding between groups. Any progress for a minority group stokes feelings of **victimhood** among the dominant population. **Law and order** politics has mass appeal, casting "us" as lawful citizens and "them," by contrast, as lawless criminals whose behavior poses an existential threat to the manhood of the nation. **Sexual anxiety** is also typical of fascist politics as the patriarchal hierarchy is threatened by growing gender equity.

As the fear of "them" grows, "we" come to represent everything virtuous. "We" live in the rural heartland, where the pure values and traditions of the nation still miraculously exist despite the threat of cosmopolitanism from the nation's cities, alongside the hordes of minorities who live there, emboldened by liberal tolerance. "We" are hardworking, and have earned our pride of place by struggle and merit. "They" are lazy, surviving off the goods we produce by exploiting the generosity of our welfare systems, or employing corrupt institutions, such as labor unions, meant to separate honest, hardworking citizens from their pay. "We" are makers; "they" are takers.

Many people are not familiar with the ideological structure of fascism, that each mechanism of fascist politics tends to build on others. They do not recognize the interconnectedness of the political slogans they are asked to repeat. I have written this book in the hope of providing citizens with the critical tools to recognize the difference between legitimate tactics in liberal democratic politics on the one hand, and invidious tactics in fascist politics on the other.

• • •

In its own history, the United States can find a legacy of the best of liberal democracy as well as the roots of fascist thought (indeed, Hitler was inspired by the Confederacy and Jim Crow laws). Following the horrors of World War II, which sent masses of refugees fleeing fascist regimes, the 1948 Universal Declaration of Human Rights affirmed the dignity of every human being. The drafting and adoption of the document were spearheaded by former First Lady Eleanor Roosevelt, and after the war it stood for the United States' ideals as much as those of the new United Nations. It was a bold statement, a powerful iteration and expansion of liberal democratic understanding of personhood to include literally the entire world community. It bound all nations and cultures to a shared commitment to valuing the equality of every person, and it rang with the aspirations of millions in a shattered world confronting the devastation of colonialism, genocide, racism, global war, and, yes, fascism. After the war, Article 14 was particularly poignant, solemnly affirming the right of every person to seek asylum. Even as the declaration attempted to prevent a repetition of the suffering experienced during World War II, it acknowledged that certain categories of people might once again have to flee the nation states under whose flag they once lived.

Fascism today might not look exactly as it did in the 1930s, but refugees are once again on the road everywhere. In multiple countries, their plight reinforces fascist propaganda that the nation is under siege, that aliens are a threat and danger both within and outside their borders. The suffering of strangers can solidify the structure of fascism. But it can also trigger empathy once another lens is clicked into place.

HOW FASCISM WORKS

1

THE MYTHIC PAST

It's in the name of tradition that the anti-Semites base their "point of view." It's in the name of tradition, the long, historical past and the blood ties with Pascal and Descartes, that the Jews are told, you will never belong here.

—Frantz Fanon, *Black Skin, White Masks* (1952)

It is only natural to begin this book where fascist politics invariably claims to discover its genesis: in the past. Fascist politics invokes a pure mythic past tragically destroyed. Depending on how the nation is defined, the mythic past may be religiously pure, racially pure, culturally pure, or all of the above. But there is a common structure to all fascist mythologizing. In all fascist mythic pasts, an extreme version of the patriarchal family reigns supreme, even just a few generations ago. Further back in time, the mythic past was a time of glory of the nation, with wars of conquest led by patriotic generals, its armies filled with its countrymen, able-bodied, loyal warriors whose wives were at home raising the next generation. In the present, these myths become the basis of the nation's identity under fascist politics.

In the rhetoric of extreme nationalists, such a glorious past has been lost by the humiliation brought on by globalism, liberal cosmopolitanism, and respect for "universal values" such as equality. These values are supposed to have made the nation weak in the face of real and threatening challenges to the nation's existence.

These myths are generally based on fantasies of a nonexistent past uniformity, which survives in the traditions of the small towns and countrysides that remain relatively unpolluted by the liberal decadence of the cities. This uniformity—linguistic, religious, geographical, or ethnic—can be perfectly ordinary in some nationalist movements, but fascist myths distinguish themselves with the creation of a glorious national history in which the members of the chosen nation ruled over others, the result of conquests and civilization-building achievements. For example, in the fascist imagination, the past invariably involves traditional, patriarchal gender roles. The fascist mythic past has a particular structure, which supports its authoritarian, hierarchical ideology. That past societies were rarely as patriarchal—or indeed as glorious—as fascist ideology represents them as being is beside the point. This imagined history provides proof to support the imposition of hierarchy in the present, and it dictates how contemporary society should look and behave.

In a 1922 speech at the Fascist Congress in Naples, Benito Mussolini declared:

> We have created our myth. The myth is a faith, a passion. It is not necessary for it to be a reality. . . . Our myth is the nation, our myth is the greatness of the nation! And to this myth, this greatness, which we want to translate into a total reality, we subordinate everything.[1]

Here, Mussolini makes clear that the fascist mythic past is *intentionally* mythical. The function of the mythic past, in fascist politics, is to harness the emotion of nostalgia to the central tenets of fascist ideology—authoritarianism, hierarchy, purity, and struggle.

With the creation of a mythic past, fascist politics creates a link between nostalgia and the realization of fascist ideals. German fascists also clearly and explicitly appreciated this point about the strategic use of a mythological past. The leading Nazi ideologue Alfred Rosenberg, editor of the prominent Nazi newspaper the *Völkischer Beobachter,* writes in 1924, "the understanding of and the respect for our own mythological past and our own history will form the first condition for more firmly anchoring the coming generation in the soil of Europe's original homeland."[2] The fascist mythic past exists to aid in *changing the present.*

. . .

The patriarchal family is one ideal that fascist politicians intend to create in society—or return to, as they claim. The patriarchal family is always represented as a central part of the nation's traditions, diminished, even recently, by the advent of liberalism and cosmopolitanism. But why is patriarchy so strategically central to fascist politics?

In a fascist society, the leader of the nation is analogous to the father in the traditional patriarchal family. The leader is the father of his nation, and his strength and power are the source of his legal authority, just as the strength and power of the father of the family in patriarchy are supposed to be the source of his ultimate moral authority over his children and wife. The leader provides for his nation, just as in the traditional family the father is the provider. The patriarchal father's authority derives from his strength, and strength is the chief authoritarian value. By representing the nation's past as one with a patriarchal family structure, fascist politics connects nostalgia to a central organizing hierarchal authoritarian structure, one that finds its purest representation in these norms.

Gregor Strasser was the National Socialist—Nazi—Reich propaganda chief in the 1920s, before the post was taken over by Joseph Goebbels. According to Strasser, "for a man, military service is the most profound and valuable form of participation—for the woman it is motherhood!"[3] Paula Siber, the acting head of the Association of German Women, in a 1933 document meant to reflect official National Socialist state policy on women, declares that "to be a woman means to be a mother, means affirming with the whole conscious force of one's soul the value of being a mother and making it a law of life . . . the highest calling of the National Socialist woman is not just to bear children, but consciously and out of total devotion to her role and duty as mother to raise children for her people."[4] Richard Grunberger, a British historian of National Socialism, sums up "the kernel of Nazi thinking on the women's question" as "a dogma of inequality between the sexes as immutable as that between the races."[5] The historian Charu Gupta, in her 1991 article "Politics of Gender: Women in Nazi Germany," goes as far as to argue that "oppression of women in Nazi Germany in fact furnishes the most extreme case of anti-feminism in the 20th century."[6]

• • •

These ideals of gender roles are defining political movements once again. In 2015, Poland's right-wing party, the Law and Justice Party (in Polish, Prawo i Sprawiedliwość, abbreviated PiS), won an outright majority in Poland's parliamentary elections, making it Poland's dominant party. PiS, in its current incarnation, has at its center a call to return to the conservative Christian social traditions of rural Poland. Most of its politicians openly abhor homosexuality. It is anti-immigrant, and the European Union has condemned its most antidemocratic measures, such as creating laws allowing government ministers (who are party members) full control of state media by granting them power to fire and hire the broadcasting chiefs of Poland's radio and television stations. But internationally it is best known for its extremism in gender politics. Abortion was already banned in Poland, with exceptions only for severe and irreversible damage to the fetus, for serious risk to the mother, or in the cases of rape or incest. The new bill proposed by PiS would have eliminated rape and incest as exceptions to the ban on abortion, with incarceration as a penalty for women who pursue the procedure. The bill failed to pass only because of a large outcry and demonstrations by women on the streets of Poland's cities.

Similar ideas about gender are on the rise globally, including in the United States, very often supported with reference to history. Andrew Auernheimer, known as weev, is a prominent neo-Nazi who ran the fascist online newspaper *The Daily Stormer* with Andrew Anglin. In May 2017, he published an article in *The Daily Stormer* titled "Just What Are Traditional Gender Roles?" In it, he claims that women were traditionally regarded as property in all European cultures, except for Jewish societies and some gypsy groups, which were matrilineal:

> This was why the Jews were so keen to attack these ideas, because the patrilineal passing of property was innately offensive to their culture. Europe only has this absurd notion of women as independent entities because of organized subversion by agents of Judaism.[7]

According to Weev, echoing twentieth-century Nazism, patriarchal gender roles are central to European history, part of the "glorious past" of white Europe.

In Weev's writing, the past not only supports traditional gender roles but separates groups that are believed to adhere to them from those that don't. From Nazi Germany to more recent history, this vindictive distinction can escalate to the point of genocide. The Hutu power movement was a fascist ethnic supremacist movement that arose in Rwanda in the years before the 1994 Rwandan genocide. In 1990, the Hutu power newspaper *Kangura* published the Hutu Ten Commandments. The first three are about gender. The first declared anyone a traitor who married a Tutsi woman, thereby polluting the pure Hutu bloodline. The third called on Hutu women to ensure that their husbands, brothers, and sons would not marry Tutsi women. The second commandment is:

> 2. Every Hutu should know that our Hutu daughters are more suitable and conscientious in their role as woman, wife and mother of the family. Are they not beautiful, good secretaries and more honest?

In Hutu power ideology, Hutu women exist only as wives and mothers, entrusted with the sacred responsibility of ensuring Hutu ethnic purity. This pursuit of ethnic purity was a key justification for killing Tutsis in the 1994 genocide.

Of course, gendered language, and references to women's roles and special value, often slip into political speech without much thought to their implication. In the 2016 U.S. election, a video surfaced showing the Republican presidential nominee Donald Trump making harshly demeaning comments about women. Mitt Romney, the Republican Party's 2012 presidential nominee, said that Trump's remarks "demean our wives and daughters." Paul Ryan, the Republican Speaker of the House, said, "women are to be championed and revered, not objectified." Both of these remarks reveal an underlying patriarchal ideology that is typical of much of U.S. Republican Party policy. These politicians could simply have given voice to the most direct description of the facts, which is that Trump's remarks demean half our fellow citizens. Instead, Romney's remark, in language evocative of that used in the Hutu Ten Commandments, describes women exclusively in terms of traditionally subordinate roles in families, as "wives and daughters"—not even as sisters. Paul Ryan's characterization of women as objects of "reverence" rather than equal respect objectifies women in the same sentence that decries doing so.

The patriarchal family in fascist politics is embedded in a larger narrative about national traditions. Hungarian prime minister Viktor Orbán was elected to office in 2010. He has overseen the demolition of the liberal institutions of that country in the service of creating what Orbán openly describes as an illiberal state. In April 2011, Orbán oversaw the introduction of "the Fundamental Law of Hungary," Hungary's new constitution. The goal of the Fundamental Law is stated at the outset, in "The National Avowal," which begins by praising the founding of the Hungarian state by Saint Stephen, who "made our country a part of Christian Europe one thousand years ago." The National Avowal continues by expressing pride that "our people has over the centuries defended Europe in a series of struggles" (presumably against the Muslim Ottoman Empire). It recognizes "the role of Christianity in preserving nationhood" and commits "to promoting and safeguarding our heritage." The National Avowal ends by promising to fulfill an "abiding need for spiritual and intellectual renewal" and to provide a way for Hungary's newer generations to "make Hungary great again."

The first series of articles in the Fundamental Law,

"The Foundation," are labeled by letters. Article L states in full:

(1) Hungary shall protect the institution of marriage as the union of a man and a woman established by voluntary decision, and the family as the basis of the survival of the nation. Family ties shall be based on marriage and/or the relationship between parents and children.
(2) Hungary shall encourage the commitment to have children.
(3) The protection of families shall be regulated by a cardinal Act.

The second series of articles, "Freedom and Responsibility," are labeled by roman numerals. Article II prohibits abortion.

The clear message is that patriarchy is a virtuous past practice whose protection from liberalism must be enshrined in the fundamental law of the country. In fascist politics, myths of a patriarchal past, threatened by encroaching liberal ideals and all that they entail, function to create a sense of panic at the loss of hierarchal status, both for men and for the dominant group's ability to protect its purity and status from foreign encroachment.

• • •

If a "return" to a patriarchal society solidifies a hierarchy in fascist politics, the source of that hierarchy reaches even deeper into the past—all the way back to Saint Stephen in the case of Hungary. In a glorious past, members of the chosen national or ethnic community realized their rightful place at the top by setting the cultural and economic agenda for everyone else. This is strategically vital. We can think of fascist politics as a politics of hierarchy (for example, in the United States, white supremacy demands and implies a perpetual hierarchy), and to realize that hierarchy, we can think of it as the displacement of reality by power. If one can convince a population that they are rightfully exceptional, that they are destined by nature or by religious fate to rule other populations, one has already convinced them of a monstrous lie.

The National Socialist movement grew out of the German *völkisch* movement, whose advocates sought a return to the traditions of a mythic German medieval past. Though Adolf Hitler was more obsessed with a certain vision of ancient Greece as a model for his Reich, leading Nazis such as Alfred Rosenberg and Heinrich Himmler, one of the most powerful members of the regime, were ardent admirers and promoters of *völkisch* thought. Bernard Mees writes in *The Science of the Swastika,* his 2008 history of the connection between German antiquarian studies and National Socialism:

> völkisch writers soon found that the picture of the ancient Germans could serve practical purposes; the glorious Germanic past could be employed as justification for the imperialist aims of the present. Hitler's desire to dominate continental Europe was explained in Nazi periodicals in the late 1930s as merely a fulfillment of Germanic destiny, repeating the prehistoric Aryan and then later Germanic migrations throughout the Continent during late antiquity.[8]

The tactics developed by Rosenberg, Himmler, and other Nazi leaders have since inspired fascist politics in other countries. According to adherents of the Hindutva movement in India, Hindus were the indigenous population of India, living according to patriarchal customs and with strict puritanical sexual practices until the arrival of Muslims, and subsequently, Christians, who introduced decadent Western values. The Hindutva movement has fabricated a version of a mythic Indian past with a pure nation of Hindus, to dramatically supplement what is regarded by scholars as the actual history of India. India's dominant nationalist party, Bharatiya Janata Party (BJP), adopted Hindutva ideology as its official creed and won power in the country using emotional rhetoric calling for a return to this fictional, patriarchal, harshly conservative, ethnically and religiously pure past. BJP is descended from the political arm of Rashtriya Swayamsevak Sangh

(RSS), an extremist, far-right Hindu nationalist party that advocated the suppression of non-Hindu minorities. Nathuram Godse, the man who assassinated Gandhi, was a member of RSS, as was current Indian prime minister Narendra Modi. RSS was explicitly influenced by European fascist movements, its leading politicians regularly praised Hitler and Mussolini in the late 1930s and 1940s.

• • •

The strategic aim of these hierarchal constructions of history is to displace truth, and the invention of a glorious past includes the erasure of inconvenient realities. While fascist politics fetishizes the past, it is never the actual past that is fetishized. These invented histories also diminish or entirely extinguish the nation's past sins. It is typical for fascist politicians to represent a country's actual history in conspiratorial terms, as a narrative concocted by liberal elites and cosmopolitans to victimize the people of the true "nation." In the United States, Confederate monuments arose well after the Civil War had ended, as part of a mythologized history of a heroic Southern past in which the horrors of slavery were de-emphasized. President Trump denounced the task of connecting of this mythologized past to slavery as an attempt to victimize white Americans for celebrating their "heritage."

Erasing the real past legitimates the vision of an ethnically pure, virtuous past nation. Part of Myanmar's ethnic cleansing of its Rohingya people is erasing any trace of their physical and historical existence. According to U Kyaw San Hla, a member of the security ministry of the Rakhine State, the traditional home of the Rohingyas, "There is no such thing as Rohingya. It is fake news."[9] According to an October 2017 report of the United Nations high commissioner for human rights, Myanmar security forces have been working to "effectively erase all signs of memorable landmarks in the geography of the Rohingya landscape and memory in such a way that a return to their lands would yield nothing but a desolate and unrecognizable terrain." What was, before 2012, a thriving multiethnic and multireligious community in certain areas of Myanmar's Rakhine State has been entirely altered to erase any memory of a Muslim population.

Fascist politics repudiates any dark moments of a nation's past. In early 2018, the Polish parliament passed a law making it illegal to suggest that Poland bore responsibility for any of the atrocities committed on its soil during the Nazi occupation of Poland, even the well-documented pogroms during this time. According to Radio Poland, "Article 55a, clause 1, of the draft law states that 'whoever accuses, publicly and against the facts, the Polish nation, or the Polish state, of being responsible or complicit in the Nazi crimes committed by the Third German Reich . . . or other crimes against peace and humanity, or war crimes, or otherwise grossly diminishes the actual perpetrators thereof, shall be subject to a fine or a penalty of imprisonment of up to three years.'" Turkey's Article 301 of its penal code outlaws "insulting Turkishness," including mentioning the Armenian genocide during the First World War. Such attempts to legislate the erasure of a nation's past are characteristic of fascist regimes.

Le Front National is France's extremist far-right party, and the first neofascist party in Western Europe to achieve significant electoral success. Its original leader, Jean-Marie Le Pen, was convicted of Holocaust denial. Le Pen's successor as leader of Le Front National is his daughter, Marine Le Pen, who finished second in the French presidential elections in 2017. The role of the French police in rounding up French Jews to be sent to Nazi death camps under the Vichy government is well documented. But during the 2017 election campaign, Marine Le Pen denied French complicity in one particularly large roundup of French Jews, in which thirteen thousand were gathered at the Vélodrome d'Hiver cycling track and sent to Nazi death camps. In a television interview in April 2017, she said: "I don't think France is responsible for the Vel' d'Hiv. . . . I think that, generally speaking, if there are people responsible, it's those who were in power at the time. It's not France." She added that the dominant liberal culture had "taught our children that they have all the reasons to criticize [the country], and to only see, perhaps, the darkest aspects of our history. So, I want them to be proud of being French again."

In Germany, where laws prevent similar, public denials of the Holocaust, the far-right party Alternativ für Deutschland (AfD) shocked the mainstream German public in the 2017 elections by becoming the third-largest party in the German parliament. During the election campaign, in September 2017, one of its party leaders, Alexander Gauland, gave a speech in which he said that "no other people have been so clearly presented with a false past as the Germans." Gauland called for "the past to be returned to the people of Germany," by which he meant a past in which Germans were free to be "proud of the accomplishments of our soldiers in both World Wars." Just as politicians in the U.S. Republican Party seek to harness white resentment (and votes) by denouncing accurate historical scholarship about the brutality of slavery as a way to "victimize" American whites, especially from the South, AfD seeks to garner votes by representing the accurate history of Germany's Nazi past as a form of victimization of the German people. In a speech earlier that year in Dresden, one of AfD's party leaders, Björn Höcke, spoke passionately about the need for "a culture of memory that brings us into contact first and foremost with the great achievements of our ancestors."[10]

Höcke's remarks about "a culture of memory" were a disturbing echo of those of the creator of Nazi Germany's myth. In 1936, Heinrich Himmler himself spoke similarly of favoring achievements:

> A people lives happily in the present and the future so long as it recognizes its past and the greatness of its ancestors. . . . We want to make it clear to our men, and to the German people, that we do not have a past of only roughly a thousand years, that we were not a barbaric people that had no culture of its own, but had to acquire it from others. We want to make our people proud again of our history.[11]

When it does not simply invent a past to weaponize the emotion of nostalgia, fascist politics cherry-picks the past, avoiding anything that would diminish unreflective adulation of the nation's glory.

• • •

In order to honestly debate what our country should do, what policies it should adopt, we need a common basis of reality, including about our own past. History in a liberal democracy must be faithful to the norm of truth, yielding an accurate vision of the past, rather than a history provided for political reasons. Fascist politics, by contrast, characteristically contains within it a demand to mythologize the past, creating a version of national heritage that is a weapon for political gain.

If one is not concerned by politicians who deliver an intentional appeal to erase painful historical memory, it is worth acquainting oneself with the psychological literature on collective memory. In their 2013 paper "Motivated to 'Forget': The Effects of In-Group Wrongdoing on Memory and Collective Guilt," Katie Rotella and Jennifer Richeson presented American participants with stories "about the oppressive, violent treatment of American Indians," framed in one of two ways: "Specifically, the perpetrators of the violence were described either as early Americans (in-group condition) or as Europeans who settled in what became America (out-group condition)."[12] The study showed that people are more likely to suffer from a sort of amnesia of wrongdoing when the perpetrators are characterized explicitly as their countrymen. When American subjects were presented with the agents of the violence as Americans (rather than Europeans), they had significantly worse memory for negative historical events, and "what participants did recall was phrased more dismissively when the perpetrators were in-group members." Rotella and Richeson's work builds on a body of previous work with similar results.[13] There already is a strong built-in bias toward forgetting and minimizing problematic acts one's in-group committed in the past. Even if politicians did nothing to stoke it, Americans would minimize the history of enslavement and genocide, Poles would minimize a history of anti-Semitism, and Turkish citizens would be inclined toward denying past atrocities against Armenians. Having politicians urge this as official educational policy adds fuel to an already raging fire.

Fascist leaders appeal to history to replace the actual historical record with a glorious mythic replacement that, in its specifics, can serve their political ends and their ultimate goal of replacing facts with power. Hungarian prime minister Viktor Orbán has drawn on Hungary's experience fighting occupation by the Ottoman Empire in the sixteenth and seventeenth centuries to represent Hungary in the historic role of defender of Christian Europe as a basis for restricting refugees today.[14] Of course, during this time, Hungary was the border between a Muslim-led empire and a Christian-led one; but religion did not play such a major role in these conflicts. (The Ottoman Empire did not, for example, demand conversion of its Christian subjects.) The mythic history Orbán tells has just enough plausibility to reduce the complex nature of the past and support his goals.

In the United States, the history of the South is continually mythologized to whitewash slavery and was used to justify the refusal to grant black U.S. citizens voting rights until a century after slavery's end. The central narrative in the justification of the South's refusal to grant blacks the vote is a false history of the period known as Reconstruction, immediately following the Civil War in 1865, when black men in the South were allowed the vote. Black Americans at that time comprised the majority in some Southern states, such as South Carolina, and for a dozen or so years their representatives had a powerful voice in many state legislatures and even occupied positions in the U.S. Congress. Reconstruction ended when Southern whites enacted laws that had the practical effect of banning black citizens from voting. White southerners propagated the myth that this was necessary because black citizens were unable to self-govern; in the histories advanced at the time, Reconstruction was represented as a time of unparalleled political corruption, with stability restored only when whites were again given full power.

W.E.B. Du Bois's 1935 masterwork, *Black Reconstruction,* is a decisive refutation of the then official history of the Reconstruction era. As Du Bois shows, whites in the South, with the collusion of Northern elites, brought an end to the Reconstruction era because of the widespread fear among the wealthy classes that newly enfranchised black citizens would join with poor whites in developing a powerful labor movement to challenge the interests of capital. Du Bois shows how the Reconstruction era was a time of just governance, when black legislators not only did not govern from their own self-interest but bent over backward to accommodate the fears of their white fellow citizens. At the time, *Black Reconstruction* was largely ignored by white historians; but by the 1960s, the history Du Bois there recounts became widely recognized as fact.

Academic historians knowingly promulgated a false history of Reconstruction for political reasons. They used their discipline not to pursue truth, but rather to address the psychic wounds of white Americans arising from the Civil War. By providing a comforting vision of history that covered over the stark moral differences between states, historians justified the removal of the minimal protections of citizenship for black citizens in former proslavery states. The final chapter of *Black Reconstruction* is titled "The Propaganda of History." In it, Du Bois harshly denounces the practice of appealing to the ideals of historical scholarship, truth and objectivity, to advance political goals. To do so, Du Bois declares, is to undermine the discipline of history. Historians who advance a false narrative for political gain under the treasured ideals of truth and objectivity, according to Du Bois, are guilty of transforming history into *propaganda*.

2

PROPAGANDA

It's hard to advance a policy that will harm a large group of people in straightforward terms. The role of political propaganda is to conceal politicians' or political movements' clearly problematic goals by masking them with ideals that are widely accepted. A dangerous, destabilizing war for power becomes a war whose aim is stability, or a war whose aim is freedom. Political propaganda uses the language of virtuous ideals to unite people behind otherwise objectionable ends.

U.S. president Richard Nixon's "war on crime" is a good example of masking problematic goals with virtuous ones. The Harvard historian Elizabeth Hinton addresses this tactic in her book *From the War on Poverty to the War on Crime: The Making of Mass Incarceration in America,* using diary notes from Nixon's chief of staff, H. R. Haldeman: "You have to face the fact that the whole problem is really the blacks," Haldeman quoted

Nixon as saying in a diary entry from April 1969. "The key is to devise a system that recognizes this while not appearing to." In a direct and systematic way, Nixon recognized that the politics of crime control could effectively conceal the racist intent behind his administration's domestic programs.[1] Nixon's rhetoric of "law and order" that followed this conversation was used to conceal a racist political agenda, one that was perfectly explicit within the White House's walls.

• • •

Fascist movements have been "draining swamps" for generations. Publicizing false charges of corruption while engaging in corrupt practices is typical of fascist politics, and anticorruption campaigns are frequently at the heart of fascist political movements. Fascist politicians characteristically decry corruption in the state they seek to take over, which is bizarre, given that fascist politicians themselves are invariably vastly more corrupt than those they seek to supplant or defeat. As the historian Richard Grunberger writes in his book *The 12-Year Reich,*

> It was a paradoxical situation. Having dinned it into the collective consciousness that democracy and corruption were synonymous, the Nazis set about constructing a governmental system beside which the scandals of the Weimar regime seemed small blemishes on the body

> politic. Corruption was in fact the central organizing principle of the Third Reich—and yet a great many citizens not only overlooked this fact, but actually regarded the men of the new regime as austerely dedicated to moral probity.[2]

. . .

Corruption, to the fascist politician, is really about the corruption of purity rather than of law. Officially, the fascist politician's denunciations of corruption sound like a denunciation of political corruption. But such talk is intended to evoke corruption in the sense of the usurpation of traditional order.

It was fabricated charges of corruption that led to the end of Reconstruction. As W.E.B. Du Bois writes in *Black Reconstruction*, "the center of the corruption charge . . . was in fact that poor men were ruling and taxing rich men."[3] And in describing the chief rhetorical claim behind disenfranchising black citizens, Du Bois writes:

> The south, finally, with almost complete unity, named the negro as the main cause of southern corruption. They said, and reiterated this charge, until it became history: that the cause of dishonesty during reconstruction was the fact that 4,000,000 disfranchised black laborers, after 250 years of exploitation, had been given a

> legal right to have some voice in their own government, in the kinds of goods they would make and the sort of work they would do, and in the distribution of the wealth which they created.[4]

To many white Americans, President Obama must have been corrupt, because his very occupation of the White House was a kind of corruption of the traditional order. When women attain positions of political power usually reserved for men—or when Muslims, blacks, Jews, homosexuals, or "cosmopolitans" profit or even share the public goods of a democracy, such as healthcare—that is perceived as corruption.[5] Fascist politicians know that their supporters will turn a blind eye to their own, true corruption since in their own case it is just a matter of members of the chosen nation taking what is rightfully theirs.

Masking corruption under the guise of anticorruption is a hallmark strategy in fascist propaganda. Vladislav Surkov was essentially Vladimir Putin's propaganda minister for many years. In his book *Nothing Is True and Everything Is Possible: The Surreal Heart of the New Russia,* the journalist Peter Pomerantsev describes Surkov's "political system in miniature" as *democratic rhetoric and undemocratic intent.*[6]

The undemocratic intent behind fascist propaganda is key. Fascist states focus on dismantling the rule of law, with the goal of replacing it with the dictates of individual rulers or party bosses. It is standard in fascist politics for harsh criticisms of an independent judiciary to occur in the form of accusations of bias, a kind of corruption, critiques that are then used to replace independent judges with ones who will cynically employ the law as a means to protect the interests of the ruling party. The recent rapid transition of certain apparently successful democratic states, such as Hungary and Poland, to nondemocratic rule has made this tactic of undermining the independent judiciary particularly salient, as both countries introduced laws to replace independent judges with party loyalists soon after antidemocratic regimes took power. Officially, the justification was that prior practices of judicial neutrality were a mask for bias against the ruling party.[7] In the name of rooting out corruption and supposed bias, fascist politicians attack and diminish the institutions that might otherwise check their power.

• • •

Just as fascist politics attacks the rule of law in the name of anticorruption, it also purports to protect freedom and individual liberties. But these liberties are contingent on the oppression of some groups. On July 5, 1852, the American abolitionist and orator Frederick Douglass delivered a Fourth of July oration in honor of that year's

Independence Day. Douglass begins his remarks by acknowledging that the day celebrates political freedom:

> This, for the purpose of this celebration, is the Fourth of July. It is the birthday of your national independence, and of your political freedom. This, to you, is what the Passover was to the emancipated people of God.[8]

Douglass spends the first part of his speech lauding the founding fathers' commitment to the cause of liberty, and praising the day as a celebration of the ideal of freedom. But then, turning to the present moment, Douglass, who was formerly enslaved, asks:

> To drag a man in fetters into the grand illuminated temple of liberty, and call upon him to join you in joyous anthems, were inhuman mockery and sacrilegious irony. Do you mean, citizens, to mock me, by asking me to speak to-day?[9]

In this famous speech, entitled "What to the Slave is the Fourth of July?," Douglass calls out the hypocrisy of a country that practices human slavery while celebrating the ideal of liberty. Americans in the nineteenth century, including those who lived in the South, regarded their land as a beacon of liberty. How is this possible, Douglass asked, when it was built by the labor of enslaved Africans and a native population whose land rights and often rights to life were thoroughly ignored? The rhetoric of liberty was effective in this situation because of a widespread belief that the native population, as well as the imported enslaved population from Africa, were not suitable recipients of the goods of liberty. This is classic fascist ideology with a hierarchy of value of worth between races. The rhetoric of liberty worked during the Confederacy by explicitly tying white southerners' liberties to the practice of slavery. When others are doing the labor for you, you are free to do as you please, at least superficially. The liberty involved in the leisurely life of the Southern planter was intimately bound up with the doctrine of white racial superiority. Under these structural conditions, the very notion of liberty in the South was predicated on its perversion in the practice of slavery. We find this inversion in much of the rhetoric of "states' rights," a phrase used to defend the liberty of U.S. states in the South from federal intervention. But the federal intervention that is most associated with the call for "states' rights" is the elimination of slavery, and subsequently Jim Crow laws restricting the right to vote for black citizens. The liberty that many whites in Southern states sought by calling for "states' rights" was the freedom to restrict the liberties of their fellow black citizens.

Historically, fascist leaders have often come to power

through democratic elections. But the commitment to freedom, such as the freedom inherent in the right to vote, tends to end with that victory. In *Mein Kampf,* after excoriating parliamentary democracy, Hitler praises "true Germanic Democracy," with "free choice of the Leader, along with his obligation to assume entire responsibility for all he does and causes to be done." What Hitler here describes is absolute rule by a leader, after an initial democratic vote. There is no suggestion in Hitler's description of what he calls "true Germanic Democracy" that the leader must subject himself to a subsequent election. (Hitler is here also drawing on the mythic past, when medieval German kings were elected for life.[10]) Whatever this system is, it is not recognizably democracy.

In the Confederacy's use of the concept of liberty to defend the practice of slavery, the Southern states' call for "states' rights" to defend slavery, and Hitler's presentation of dictatorial rule as democracy, liberal democratic ideals are used as a mask to undermine themselves. In each we can find specious arguments that the antiliberal goal is in fact a realization of the liberal ideal. In the case of the Confederacy and the Jim Crow U.S. South, the argument was that "states' rights," a manifestation of the liberal ideal of self-determination, allowed for the practice of racial subordination, as this was a choice made by each state. Hitler argues that "true Germanic Democracy"—that is, dictatorship by a single individual—is genuine democracy because only in such a system does genuine individual responsibility for political decisions exist, as the power to make those decisions rests with one person—and individual responsibility is a liberal notion par excellence.

. . .

In book 8 of Plato's *Republic,* Socrates argues that people are not naturally led to self-governance but rather seek a strong leader to follow. Democracy, by permitting freedom of speech, opens the door for a demagogue to exploit the people's need for a strongman; the strongman will use this freedom to prey on the people's resentments and fears. Once the strongman seizes power, he will end democracy, replacing it with tyranny. In short, book 8 of *The Republic* argues that democracy is a self-undermining system whose very ideals lead to its own demise.

Fascists have always been well acquainted with this recipe for using democracy's liberties against itself; Nazi propaganda minister Joseph Goebbels once declared, "This will always remain one of the best jokes of democracy, that it gave its deadly enemies the means by which it was destroyed." Today is no different from the past. Again, we find the enemies of liberal democracy employing this strategy, pushing the freedom of speech to its limits and ultimately using it to subvert others' speech.

Desiree Fairooz is a former librarian and activist who was present at the confirmation hearing of U.S. attorney general Jeff Sessions. Sessions is a former Alabama senator whose nomination to the federal bench had been rejected by the U.S. Senate in 1986 over accusations of far-right extremism, particularly racism (as a senator, Sessions had made a name for himself by fomenting panic about immigration). When Senator Richard Shelby of Alabama declared that Sessions had a "well-documented record of treating all Americans equally under the law," Fairooz chuckled. She was immediately arrested and charged with disruptive and disorderly conduct. The Justice Department, headed by Sessions, pressed charges against her. After a judge dismissed the charges in the summer of 2017 on the grounds that laughter is permitted speech, Sessions's Justice Department decided in September 2017 to continue to pursue charges against her; it was not until November of that year that the Justice Department abandoned its attempt to bring Fairooz to trial for chuckling.

U.S. attorney general Jeff Sessions is hardly a defender of free speech. And yet the very same month that his Justice Department was again attempting to bring an American citizen to trial for laughing, Sessions delivered a speech at Georgetown Law School excoriating university campuses for failing to live up to a commitment to free speech because of the presumption that the academy discourages right-leaning voices. He called for a "national recommitment to free speech and the First Amendment" (in the week Sessions gave this speech, news was dominated by President Trump's call for the owners of National Football League teams to fire players who knelt during the national anthem to protest racism, an exercise of First Amendment rights if ever there was one).

United States politics has recently been dominated by pro-free-speech rhetoric from far-right nationalists. The regular pro-Trump rallies in Portland, Oregon, are called "Trump Free Speech Rallies." In May 2017, the city was the site of a particularly brutal white nationalist terrorist act when Jeremy Joseph Christian, a thirty-five-year-old far-right nationalist, allegedly stabbed three people who tried to intervene as he was hurling anti-Muslim insults at two young women. Two of the stabbing victims died from their injuries. When entering the courtroom to be arraigned, Christian shouted:

> Free speech or die, Portland! You got no safe place. This is America. Get out if you don't like free speech. You call it terrorism, I call it patriotism.[11]

The chief reason we have free speech in democracy is to facilitate public discourse about policy on the part of citizens and their representatives. But the kind of debate where one shrieks insults at another, not to mention engages in physical violence and then denounces protest as an attack on speech, is not the relevant kind of public discourse that free speech rights are meant to protect.

The kind of speech that Jeremy Joseph Christian wished to engage in destroys the possibility of, rather than facilitates, public discourse.

It is often noted, rightly, that fascism elevates the irrational over the rational, fanatical emotion over the intellect. It is less often remarked upon, however, that fascism performs this elevation indirectly, that is to say, propagandistically. "The Rhetoric of Hitler's 'Battle'" is a 1939 essay by the American literary theorist Kenneth Burke. In it, Burke describes how Hitler, in *Mein Kampf,* repeatedly describes his struggle to embrace National Socialist ideals, such as the realization that life is a battle for power between groups in which reason and objectivity have no role, his realization that humans are beasts, and his rejection of the Enlightenment, as *driven* by reason. Burke writes, "those who attack Hitlerism as a cult of the irrational should emend their statements to this extent: irrational it is, but it is carried on under the *slogan* of 'Reason.'" Fascists reject Enlightenment ideals while proclaiming that they are forced to do so by a stark confrontation with reality, by the natural law. As Burke notes, Hitler describes his transition into a "fanatical anti-Semite" as "a struggle of 'reason' and 'reality' against his 'heart.'" The fascist claims to have been driven by scientific reason to the view that life is a merciless struggle for dominance, in which the very force that has allegedly brought him to this—the enlightenment ideal of universal reason—must be abandoned.

3

ANTI-INTELLECTUAL

Fascist politics seeks to undermine public discourse by attacking and devaluing education, expertise, and language. Intelligent debate is impossible without an education with access to different perspectives, a respect for expertise when one's own knowledge gives out, and a rich enough language to precisely describe reality. When education, expertise, and linguistic distinctions are undermined, there remains only power and tribal identity.

This does not mean that there is no role for universities in fascist politics. In fascist ideology, there is only one legitimate viewpoint, that of the dominant nation. Schools introduce students to the dominant culture and its mythic past. Education therefore either poses a grave threat to fascism or becomes a pillar of support for the mythical nation. It's no wonder, then, that protests and cultural clashes on campuses represent a true political battleground and receive national attention. The stakes are high.

. . .

For at least the past fifty years, universities have been the epicenter of protest against injustice and authoritarian overreach. Consider, for example, their unique role in the antiwar movement of the 1960s. Where speech is a right, propagandists cannot attack dissent head-on; instead they must represent it as something violent and oppressive (a protest therefore becomes a "riot"). In 2015, the Black Lives Matter movement in the United States, protesting police brutality and racial inequality, spread to university campuses. Given that Black Lives Matter began in Ferguson, Missouri, it is no surprise that the first campus it touched was the University of Missouri. Concernedstudent1950 was the name of the Missouri student movement, named to evoke the year in which the University of Missouri was desegregated. Among its aims was to address the incidents of racial abuse that black students faced on a regular basis, as well as addressing curricula that represented culture and civilization as the product solely of white men. The media largely ignored these motivations and, representing protesting black students as an angry mob, used the situation as an opportunity to foment rage against the supposed liberal political excesses of the university.

Fascist politics seeks to undermine the credibility of institutions that harbor independent voices of dissent until they can be replaced by media and universities that reject those voices. One typical method is to level accusations of hypocrisy. Right now, a contemporary right-wing campaign is charging universities with hypocrisy on the issue of free speech. Universities, they say, claim to hold free speech in the highest regard but suppress any voices that don't lean left by allowing protests against them on campus. Most recently, critics of campus social justice movements have found an effective method of turning themselves into the victims of protest. They contend that protesters mean to deny them their own free speech.

These accusations extend into the classroom. David Horowitz is a far-right activist who has been targeting universities, and the film industry, since the 1980s. In 2006, Horowitz published a book, *The Professors*, naming the "101 most dangerous professors in America," a list of leftist and liberal professors, many of whom were supporters of Palestinian rights. In 2009, he published another book, *One-Party Classroom*, with a list of the "150 most dangerous courses in America."

Horowitz has created numerous organizations to promote his ideas. In the 1990s, Horowitz created the Individual Rights Foundation, which, according to the conservative Young America's Foundation, "led the battle against speech codes on college campuses." In 1992, he founded the monthly tabloid *Heterodoxy,* which, according to the Southern Poverty Law Center, "targeted university students whom Horowitz viewed as being indoctrinated by the entrenched Left in American academia." Horowitz is also responsible for Students for Academic Freedom, which was called the Campaign for Fairness and Inclusion in Higher Education when it was introduced in 2003. The goal of Students for Academic Freedom is to promote the hiring of professors with conservative worldviews, an effort marketed as promoting "intellectual diversity and academic freedom at America's colleges and universities," according to Young America's Foundation. For the past several decades, Horowitz was a fringe figure on the American far right. More recently, his tactics and aims, and even his rhetoric, have moved into the mainstream, where attacks on "political correctness" on campuses are now commonplace.

The Trump administration has aggressively pursued Horowitz's agenda. Deputy associate attorney general of the U.S. Department of Justice, Jesse Panuccio, began a speech at Northwestern University on January 26, 2018, by declaring campus free speech "a vitally important topic, and, as you are probably aware, one that Attorney General Sessions has made a priority for the Department of Justice. It is a priority because, in our view, many campuses across the country are failing to protect and promote free speech."

Trump's presidential campaign is sometimes described as one long attack on "political correctness."[1] It is not accidental that the rhetoric of the Trump administration, in particular its attacks on "political correctness" and its use of free-speech rhetoric, overlaps with the talking points of some of the well-funded institutions that have arisen to attack and delegitimize universities as bastions of liberalism. There are links between Horowitz's main organization, the David Horowitz Freedom Center (DHFC), and the Trump administration, especially with its members on the far right. According to an investigation by the *Washington Post* published in June 2017, the DHFC has supported political operatives whose aim has been to destabilize establishment Washington politics, tilting it to the far right, including Attorney General Jeff Sessions, senior policy adviser Stephen Miller, and Stephen Bannon.[2] According to the article, on December 14, 2016, "Horowitz expressed happiness about Trump's victory and said Republicans had finally woken up to his approach to politics," denouncing leftists as enemies of free speech.

Horowitz counts at least eleven (onetime) members of the Trump administration as supporters of the DHFC, including Vice President Mike Pence, Sessions, Bannon, and Miller, whom Horowitz legitimately describes as "a kind of protégé of mine" (the article documents Horowitz's lengthy support for Miller's career). The center has been deeply involved in the careers of senior Trump administrative officials for many years, and according to the *Post*'s investigation has long served as a sort of informal gathering place for the far-right members of the administration.

Horowitz's free speech attacks on universities lack legitimacy. Given the formal protections of academic freedom, universities in the United States host the freest domain of expression of any workplace. In private workplaces in the United States, free speech is a fantasy. Workers are regularly subjected to nondisclosure agreements, forbidding them to speak about various matters. In most workplaces, workers can be fired for political speech on social media. Attacking the only workplaces in a country with genuine free-speech protections using the ideal of free speech is another instance of the familiar Orwellian nature of propaganda.

In January 2017, Missouri state representative Rick Brattin amended a bill he had previously introduced to the state legislature to ban tenure at all of Missouri's public universities. After calling tenure "un-American" in an interview with *The Chronicle of Higher Education,* Brattin added, "Something's wrong, something's broken, and a professor that should be educating our kids, should be concentrating on ensuring that they're propelling to a better future, but instead are engaging in political stuff that they shouldn't be engaged in. Because they have tenure, they're allowed to do so. And that is wrong."[3] When Brattin was asked whether he was concerned that eliminating tenure would damage academic freedom and lead to professors losing their jobs for political reasons, he responded by asking in what other profession people have that freedom and why academia should be a special case. The work that scholars produce may necessarily have political implications, depending on the field. Attacks from the right make clear the right wing's own desire to control acceptable lines of inquiry. In the classic style of demagogic propaganda, the tactic of attacking institutions standing up for public reason and open debate occurs under the cloak of those very ideals.

. . .

Within universities, fascist politicians target professors they deem too political—typically, too Marxist—and denounce entire areas of study. When fascist movements are under way in liberal democratic states, certain academic disciplines are singled out. Gender studies, for instance, comes under fire from far-right nationalist movements across the world. The professors and teachers in these fields are accused of disrespect to the traditions of the nation.

Whenever fascism threatens, its representatives and facilitators denounce universities and schools as sources of "Marxist indoctrination," the classic bogeyman of fascist politics. Typically used without any connection to Marx or Marxism, the expression is employed in fascist politics as a way to malign equality. That is why universities that seek to give some intellectual space to marginalized perspectives, however small, are subject to denunciation as hotbeds of "Marxism." Fascism is about the dominant perspective, and so, during fascist moments, there is strong support for figures to denounce disciplines that teach perspectives other than the dominant ones—such as gender studies or, in the United States, African American studies or Middle Eastern studies. The dominant perspective is often misrepresented as the truth, the "real history," and any attempt to allow a space for alternative perspectives is derided as "cultural Marxism."

Fascist opposition to gender studies, in particular, flows from its patriarchal ideology. National Socialism targeted women's movements and feminism generally; for the Nazis, feminism was a Jewish conspiracy to destroy fertility among Aryan women. Charu Gupta aptly summarizes the Nazi attitude toward feminist movements:

> [Nazis] believed that the women's movement was part of an international Jewish conspiracy to subvert the German family and thus destroy the German race. The

> movement, it claimed, was encouraging women to assert their economic independence and to neglect their proper task of producing children. It was spreading the feminine doctrines of pacifism, democracy and "materialism." By encouraging contraception and abortion and so lowering the birth rate, it was attacking the very existence of the German people.[4]

In fascist attacks on universities, the universities play the role of the Nazi "Jewish conspiracy" behind the women's movement. Universities subvert masculinity and undermine the traditional family by supporting gender studies.

In Russia, Vladimir Putin has gone on the offensive on this issue, repurposing universities into ideological weapons directed against the supposed Western excesses of feminism. In her 2017 book, *The Future Is History: How Totalitarianism Reclaimed Russia*, the journalist Masha Gessen describes how Russia's antigay, antifeminist university agenda emerged out of a 1997 conference in Prague called the World Congress of Families, organized by Allan Carlson, an American historian at the "ultraconservative Hillsdale College in Michigan." The conference had a large turnout. Gessen writes, "Inspired by the turnout, the organizers turned the World Congress of Families into a permanent organization dedicated to the fight against gay rights, abortion rights, and gender studies."[5]

As one example of policies inspired by the conference, the Russian government persecuted the European University of St. Petersburg for its liberal inclinations; Russian authorities have been trying to close it down for years and finally succeeded in 2016, when its teaching license was suspended. According to the university, "the inspections were instigated by an official complaint from Vitaly Milonov," a member of the Russian parliament for Vladimir Putin's United Russia Party, who is responsible for some of Russia's extreme antigay legislation. Milonov expressed concern about the teaching of gender studies at the university. "I personally find that disgusting, it's fake studies, and it may well be illegal," Mr. Milonov told the *Christian Science Monitor.*[6] In Hungary and Poland, gender studies has also been a flash point of political controversy, drawing the ire of political leaders seeking to paint universities as bastions of liberal indoctrination. As Andrea Pető relates in her study "Report from the Trenches: The Debate Around Teaching Gender Studies in Hungary," the undersecretary of the Hungarian Ministry of Human Resources, Bence Rétvári, compared gender studies to Marxist-Leninism (again, the standard bogeyman of fascist regimes).

As in Russia and Eastern Europe, attacking gender studies is an explicit part of the far-right movement in the United States. In 2010, the state legislature of North Carolina was taken over by Republicans affiliated with the far-right "Tea Party" movement. Together with the Republican governor, Pat McCrory, they went after the distinguished institution the University of North Carolina. A newly appointed Board of Governors of the university dismissed its widely admired progressive president, Tom Ross. Governor McCrory said in an interview that public universities should not teach courses in "gender studies or Swahili" (Swahili is an African language spoken by 140 million people as a first or second language). McCrory added, "If you want to take gender studies, that's fine, go to a private school and take it."

Some will argue that a university must have representatives of *all* positions and that changes such as those made in North Carolina merely make room for opposing perspectives. These arguments rest on the grounds that being justified in our own positions requires regularly grappling with opposing ones (as well as on the grounds that there was no room in the first place). Anyone who has taught philosophy knows that it is often useful to confront cogent defenses of opposing positions, and universities unquestionably benefit from intelligent and sophisticated proponents of positions along the political spectrum. Nevertheless, the general principle in these instances is not, upon reflection, particularly plausible.

No one thinks that the demands of free inquiry require adding researchers to university faculties who seek to demonstrate that the earth is flat. Such a position we have determined through conclusive scientific inquiry to be fruitless. Even the most ardent defender of free speech does not argue that we should spend precious university resources on this question. Adding a flat earther would, rather, impede objective inquiry. Similarly, I can safely and justifiably reject ISIS ideology without having to confront its advocates in the classroom or faculty lounge. I do not need to have a colleague who defends the view that Jewish people are genetically predisposed to greed in order to justifiably reject such anti-Semitic nonsense. Nor is it even remotely plausible that adding such voices to the faculty lounge would aid arguments against such toxic ideologies. More likely, so doing would undermine intelligent debate by leading to breakdowns of communication and shouting matches.

Fascist politics, however, makes room for the study of myths as fact. In fascist ideology, the function of the education system is to glorify the mythic past, elevating the achievements of members of the nation and obscuring the perspectives and histories of those who do not belong. In a process sometimes tendentiously called "decolonizing" the curriculum, neglected perspectives are incorporated, thereby ensuring that students have a full view of history's actors. In the fight against fascism, adjusting the curriculum in this way is not mere "political correctness." Representing the voices of all of those whose existence has shaped and formed the world in which we live provides an essential means of protection against fascist myth.

• • •

In fascist ideology, the goal of general education in the schools and universities is to instill pride in the mythic past; fascist education extols academic disciplines that reinforce hierarchal norms and national tradition. For the fascist, schools and universities are there to indoctrinate national or racial pride, conveying for example (where nationalism is racialized) the glorious achievements of the dominant race.

Governor McCrory did not stop with his suggestion that some courses should be removed from the public curriculum. He also called on the university to focus more on the type of skills-based education that employers supposedly need, to the detriment of subjects like sociology, which aid students in becoming better democratic citizens. He was backed up by the Pope Center for Higher Education Policy, run and funded by Art Pope, North Carolina's immensely powerful and wealthy Republican donor, which has successfully urged the University of North Carolina to raise its tuition. As Pope incisively recognizes, this move will lead more students away from humanities and social sciences and into majors that will give them "business skills."

At the same time that it denigrates teaching subjects

that would enable a greater understanding of human cultural diversity, the Pope Center for Higher Education Policy (now known as the James G. Martin Center for Academic Renewal) urges the teaching of a "Great Books" curriculum, which emphasizes the cultural achievements of white Europeans.[7] The priorities here make sense when one realizes that in antidemocratic systems, the function of education is to produce obedient citizens structurally obliged to enter the workforce without bargaining power, and ideologically trained to think that the dominant group represents history's greatest civilizational forces. Conservative figures pour huge sums into the project of advancing right-wing goals in education. For example, in 2017 the Charles Koch Foundation, just one of the conservative foundations in the United States funded by right-wing oligarchs, alone spent $100 million to support projects largely devoted to conservative ideology at around 350 colleges and universities, according to some sources.[8]

In fascist ideology, the products of intellectual life that it supports—culture, civilization, and art—are solely productions of members of the chosen nation. When universities restrict their required offerings to the European cultural touchstones, they risk suggesting that white Europeans constitute the core of human civilization. It should give fans of such "Great Books" programs pause that Hitler declares in *Mein Kampf* that "all that we admire on this earth—science, art, technical skill and invention—is the creative product of only a small number of nations. . . . All this culture depends on them for its very existence. . . . If we divide the human race into three categories—founders, maintainers, and destroyers of culture—the Aryan stock alone can be considered as representing the first category." Our universities must not be complicit, even unwittingly, in promulgating such fascist myths.

Across time and place, as fascism rises, so, too, do figures who call for stacking the schools and universities with teachers more sympathetic to the nationalist or traditionalist ideals. What has been happening in Hungary is a classic example. When Viktor Orbán assumed power, he condemned the schools as sites for liberal indoctrination. He nationalized the school system, which was previously under local school board control, and introduced a professional organization that all teachers had to join, which bound them to serve "in the interests of the nation." A new national core curriculum recommended the work of anti-Semitic Hungarian writers. Schools were told to encourage activities evocative of a glorious mythic Hungarian national past, such as horseback riding and the singing of Hungarian folk songs.

The best university in Hungary is Central European University (CEU), which retains independence from the Hungarian state. Orbán presents CEU as a foreign institution that seeks to displace local Hungarian schools, spreading liberal universalist values such as pro-immigration sentiment. In April 2017, the Hungarian parliament attached legislation to an anti-immigration bill seeking to strip CEU of its ability to operate as an American university in Hungary and regulating the movement of its faculty and students for national security reasons. As a consequence, CEU might close its doors in Hungary.

Similar efforts to shape curricula to nationalist ends are under way around the world, including in Turkey, where one of the first actions Turkey's president Recep Tayyip Erdoğan undertook after the attempted coup against him in 2016 was to dismiss more than five thousand deans and academics from their posts in Turkish universities for suspicion of pro-democratic or pro-leftist sentiments. Many were also imprisoned. In an interview with Voice of America for a February 2017 article, İsmet Akça, a political science professor who was removed from his position at Istanbul Yildiz Technical University, said, "These people being purged are not just democratic left-oriented people, they are very good scientists, very good academics. By purging them, the government is also attacking the very idea of the higher education, the very idea of the universities in this country."[9] In 2017, after winning a national referendum giving him new, sweeping, almost dictatorial powers, Erdoğan introduced a new educational curriculum for the schools. Its goal was to de-emphasize secular ideals and eliminate scientific theories that run counter to religious ideology, such as evolution. The education ministry declared that Turkey's history would be taught "from the perspective of a national and moral education," with the aim of protecting "national values," rather than reflecting the secular liberal ideals that had been at the center of Turkish civil society, including its education system, since Kemal Atatürk.

. . .

The far-right American radio host Rush Limbaugh has, on his popular radio show, denounced "the four corners of deceit: government, academia, science and media. Those institutions are now corrupt and exist by virtue of deceit. That's how they promulgate themselves; it is how they prosper."[10] Limbaugh, here, provides a perfect example of how fascist politics targets *expertise,* mocking and devaluing it. In liberal democracy, political leaders are supposed to consult with those they represent, as well as with experts and scientists who can most accurately explain the demands of reality on policy.

Fascist leaders are instead "men of action" with no use for consultation or deliberation. In his 1941 essay "The Rebirth of European Man," the French fascist Pierre Drieu la Rochelle writes, "It is a type of man who rejects culture. . . . It is a man who does not believe in ideas, and hence rejects doctrines. It is a man who only believes in acts and carries out these acts in line with a nebulous myth."[11] Once universities and experts have been delegitimized, fascist politicians are free to create their own realities, shaped by their own individual will. Limbaugh has been attacking science for many years, proclaiming that "science has become a home for displaced socialists and communists." In the current moment in U.S. politics, when climate science is mocked and derided by Trump and his administration, we see the triumph of the disparagement of scientific expertise.

By rejecting the value of expertise, fascist politicians also remove any requirement for sophisticated debate. Reality is always more complex than our means of representing it. Scientific language requires ever more complex terminology, to make distinctions that would be invisible without it. Social reality is at least as complex as the reality of physics. In a healthy liberal democracy, a public language with a rich and varied vocabulary to make distinctions is a vital democratic institution. Without it, healthy public discourse is impossible. Fascist politics seeks to degrade and debase the language of politics; fascist politics thereby seeks to mask reality.

Victor Klemperer's 1947 work *The Language of the Third Reich* is about the language of National Socialism, which he calls LTI (short for Lingua Tertii Imperii). Chapter 3, entitled "Distinguishing Feature: Poverty," begins, "The LTI is destitute. Its poverty is a fundamental one; it is as if it had sworn a vow of poverty." Adolf Hitler was very explicit about the importance of impoverishing public discourse in this manner. In his chapter on propaganda in *Mein Kampf,* he writes:

> All propaganda should be popular and should adapt its intellectual level to the receptive ability of the least intellectual of those whom it is desired to address. Thus it must sink its mental elevation deeper in proportion to the numbers of the mass whom it has to grip. . . . The receptive ability of the masses is very limited, and their understanding small; on the other hand, they have a great power of forgetting. This being so, all effective propaganda must be confined to very few points which must be brought out in the form of slogans.[12]

In a healthy liberal democracy, language is a tool of information. The goal of fascist propaganda is not merely to mock and sneer at robust and complex public debate about policy; it is to eliminate its possibility. According to Klemperer,

> every language able to assert itself freely fulfils all human needs, it serves reason as well as emotion, it is communication and conversation, soliloquy and prayer, plea, command, and invocation. The LTI only serves the

> cause of invocation. . . . The sole purpose of LTI is to strip everyone of their individuality, to paralyze them as personalities, to make them into unthinking and docile cattle in a herd driven and hounded in a particular direction, to turn them into atoms in a huge rolling block of stone. The LTI is the language of mass fanaticism.[13]

It is a core tenet of fascist politics that the goal of oratory should not be to convince the intellect, but to sway the will. The anonymous author of an article in a 1925 Italian fascist magazine writes, "The mysticism of Fascism is the proof of its triumph. Reasoning does not attract, emotion does."[14] In *Mein Kampf,* in a chapter entitled "The Struggle in the Early Days: The Role of the Orator," Hitler writes that it is a gross misunderstanding to dismiss simple language as stupid. Throughout *Mein Kampf,* Hitler is clear that the aim of propaganda is to replace reasoned argument in the public sphere with irrational fears and passions. In a February 2018 interview, Steve Bannon said, "We got elected on Drain the Swamp, Lock Her Up, Build a Wall. . . . This was pure anger. Anger and fear is what gets people to the polls."[15]

Across the world right now, we see far-right movements attacking universities for spreading "Marxism" and "feminism" and failing to give a central place to far-right values. Even in the United States, home to the world's greatest university system, we see Eastern European–style attacks on universities. Student protests are misrepresented in the press as riots by undisciplined mobs, threats to the civil order. In fascist politics, universities are debased in public discourse, and academics are undermined as legitimate sources of knowledge and expertise, represented as radical "Marxists" or "feminists" spreading a leftist ideological agenda under the guise of research. By debasing institutions of higher learning and impoverishing our joint vocabulary to discuss policy, fascist politics reduces debate to ideological conflict. Via such strategies, fascist politics degrades information spaces, occluding reality.

4

UNREALITY

When propaganda succeeds at twisting ideals against themselves and universities are undermined and condemned as sources of bias, reality itself is cast into doubt. We can't agree on truth. Fascist politics replaces reasoned debate with fear and anger. When it is successful, its audience is left with a destabilized sense of loss, and a well of mistrust and anger against those who it has been told are responsible for this loss.

Fascist politics exchanges reality for the pronouncements of a single individual, or perhaps a political party. Regular and repeated obvious lying is part of the process by which fascist politics destroys the information space. A fascist leader can replace truth with power, ultimately lying without consequence. By replacing the world with a person, fascist politics makes us unable to assess arguments by a common standard. The fascist politician possesses specific techniques to destroy information spaces and break down reality.

. . .

Anyone looking at current U.S. politics, or current Russian politics, or current Polish politics, would immediately note the presence and political potency of *conspiracy theories*.

The task of defining conspiracy theories presents difficult issues. The philosopher Giulia Napolitano has suggested that we should think of conspiracy theories as "aimed" at some out-group, and in the service of some in-group. Conspiracy theories function to denigrate and delegitimize their targets, by connecting them, mainly symbolically, to problematic acts. Conspiracy theories do not function like ordinary information; they are, after all, often so outlandish that they can hardly be expected to be literally believed. Their function is rather to raise general suspicion about the credibility and the decency of their targets.

Conspiracy theories are a critical mechanism used to delegitimize the mainstream media, which fascist politicians accuse of bias for failing to cover false conspiracies. Perhaps the most famous twentieth-century conspiracy theory revolves around *The Protocols of the Elders of Zion*, which was at the basis of Nazi ideology. *The Protocols* is an early-twentieth-century hoax, supposedly written as an instruction manual to Jews as a plot for world domination. Scholars have discovered that it was liberally plagiarized from Maurice Joly's 1864 book, *A Dialogue in Hell Between Machiavelli and Montesquieu,* a political satire set as a debate in hell between Montesquieu, who makes the case for liberalism, and Machiavelli, who makes the case for tyranny. Machiavelli's arguments for tyranny are transformed, in *The Protocols,* into arguments made by the "Elders of Zion," supposedly Jewish leaders bent on world domination. It appears to have been published for the first time as an appendix to the Russian author and religious mystic Sergei Nilus's 1905 book, *The Anti-Christ.* In 1906, it was published serially in a St. Petersburg newspaper under the title "The Conspiracy, or The Roots of the Disintegration of European Society." In 1907, it appeared as a book, published by the St. Petersburg Society for the Deaf and Dumb. It sold millions of copies throughout the world in the 1920s, including in the United States, where half a million copies were mass-produced and distributed by Henry Ford, the automaker, by 1925.

According to *The Protocols,* Jews are at the center of a global conspiracy that dominates the most respected mainstream media outlets and the global economic system, using them to spread democracy, capitalism, and communism, all masks for Jewish interests. The most prominent and influential Nazi leaders, including Hitler and Goebbels, firmly believed this conspiracy theory to be true. Throughout Nazi writings, we find denunciations of the "Jewish press" for failure to denounce or even mention the international Jewish conspiracy.

The 2016 U.S. presidential election was marred by a series of conspiracy theories. These were aimed against several targets, including Hillary Clinton, the Democratic candidate, as well as Muslims and refugees. Perhaps the most bizarre such theory was "Pizzagate." According to those who spread it, leaked emails from John Podesta, Clinton's campaign manager, were said to spell out secret coded messages about the trafficking of young children for sex to Democratic congressmen, conducted from a pizzeria in Washington, D.C. The theories were circulated on social media and, given their bizarre nature, achieved surprisingly wide currency. Though it was just one among several bizarre conspiracy theories about Clinton and the Democrats, it received outsized national attention, not just for its extreme oddity but because Edgar Maddison Welch, a man from North Carolina, actually showed up, gun in hand, at the pizzeria to confront its owners and free the supposed sexual slaves. The goal of this conspiracy was to connect its targets, Democrats, to acts of extreme depravity.

The University of Connecticut philosopher Michael Lynch has used the example of "Pizzagate" as evidence for the thesis that conspiracy theories are not intended to be treated as ordinary information. Lynch points out that if one were actually supposed to believe that there was a pizzeria in Washington, D.C., that was trafficking in child sex slaves for Democratic congressmen, it would be entirely rational to act as Edger Maddison Welch acted. And yet, Welch was roundly *condemned* by those who promulgated the "Pizzagate" conspiracy for his actions. Lynch's point is that the "Pizzagate" conspiracy was not intended to be treated as ordinary information. The function of conspiracy theories is to impugn and malign their targets, but not necessarily by convincing their audience that they are true. In the case of "Pizzagate," the conspiracy theory was intended to remain at the level of innuendo and slander.

Donald Trump came to mainstream political attention by attacking the press for their supposed censorship of the conspiracy theory called "birtherism," the belief that President Obama was born in Kenya and therefore not eligible to be president of the United States. In an interview with CNN on May 29, 2012, Trump railed at Wolf Blitzer and CNN for not covering the topic, because, according to Trump, they were working for Obama. Fox News, in contrast, provided Trump a ready platform to promote his conspiracy theories. President Trump is not an outlier here; conspiracy theories are the calling cards of fascist politics. Conspiracy theories are tools to attack those who would ignore their existence; by not covering them, the media is made to appear biased and ultimately part of the very conspiracy they refuse to cover.

Conspiracy theories not only have the power to influence perceptions of reality, they can also shape the course of real events. Poland's ruling far-right party, PiS, is best known for its social conservatism and its disdain for liberal democratic institutions. But it is less often noted outside Poland that PiS came to power on the wings of conspiracy theories every bit as fantastical as the "birtherism" conspiracy that ushered Donald Trump into the mainstream of U.S. politics, and eventually the presidency.

On April 10, 2010, a plane carrying Polish president Lech Kaczynski and the first lady, as well as the entire General Army Command of the Polish Armed Forces, the president of the National Bank, and many other members of the Polish political elite, crashed in a forest while attempting a landing at the airport in Smolensk, Russia. The delegation was on the way to commemorate the seventieth anniversary of the Katyn massacre, where the Soviet Secret Police executed more than twenty thousand members of the Polish officer corps. The crash of the airplane was a national tragedy for Poland. Commissions assigned to investigate its causes in Russia and Poland, as well as the available cockpit voice recorder transcripts, determined that pilot error was to blame.

However, soon after the crash, prominent politicians

in PiS began to question the official narratives emerging from the Russian and Polish investigative commissions. PiS's strategy in the immediate aftermath was to implicate Poland's moderate government as well as the Russian government in a conspiracy to down the aircraft and cover up the crime. Figures associated with PiS have floated about twenty different conspiracy theories about the crash. The mainstream press would denounce the "Smolensk Sect" as conspiracy theorists who were attempting to divide the country, a characterization that those who promulgated the conspiracy theories would in turn use to malign and impugn the press for bias. PiS's ultimate parliamentary success came from how it used these conspiracy theories to undermine faith in the country's primary democratic institutions, the government and the press.

Fascist politicians discredit the "liberal media" for censoring discussion of outlandish right-wing conspiracy theories, which suggests mendacious behavior covered up by the veneer of liberal democratic institutions. Conspiracy theories play to the most paranoid elements of society—in the case of the United States, fear of foreign elements and Islam (as in the "birther" theory that President Barack Obama was born a Muslim in Kenya); in the case of Hungary and Poland, anti-Semitism and anticommunism. The goal of the conspiracies is to cause widespread mistrust and paranoia, justifying drastic measures, such as censoring or shutting down the "liberal" media and imprisoning "enemies of the state."

George Soros is an American billionaire philanthropist of Hungarian Jewish origin. Soros's philanthropic organization, the Open Society Foundations, has been deeply involved in democracy-building efforts in more than a hundred countries, including in his native Hungary, where his support also led to the founding of Central European University, Hungary's leading university. In 2017, Hungarian prime minister Viktor Orbán claimed that there was a "Soros Plan" to flood Hungary with non-Christian migrants in order to dilute the nation's Christian identity. Orbán's government has launched a campaign against George Soros and his alleged plan, including billboards and television ads targeting Soros, employing what many have perceived to be starkly anti-Semitic representations. There is of course no evidence whatsoever that the Jewish financier has any sort of plan to flood Hungary with non-Christian migrants, but the lack of evidence in the mainstream media is taken, by the Orbán government, to be evidence of Soros's control over it, when in fact it is Orbán who is manipulating reality.

Hannah Arendt, perhaps the twentieth century's greatest theorist of totalitarianism, gave clear warning of the importance of conspiracy theories in antidemocratic politics. In *The Origins of Totalitarianism,* she writes:

> Mysteriousness as such became the first criterion for the choice of topics. . . . The effectiveness of this kind of propaganda demonstrates one of the chief characteristics of modern masses. They do not believe in anything visible, in the reality of their own experience; they do not trust their eyes and ears but only their imaginations, which may be caught by anything that is at once universal and consistent in itself. What convinces masses are not facts, and not even invented facts, but only the consistency of the system of which they are presumably part. Repetition . . . is only important because it convinces them of consistency in time.[1]

Because the audience for conspiracy theories readily discount their own experience, it is often unimportant that the conspiracy theories are demonstrably false. Texas House Bill 45, the "American Laws for American Courts" bill signed into law by Texas governor Greg Abbott in June 2017, is intended to block Muslims from bringing Sharia law into the state. That Muslims are trying to sneakily transform Texas into an Islamic republic is deeply improbable—as is the hypothesis that President Obama is a secret Muslim pretending to be a Christian in order to overthrow the U.S. government. These conspiracy theories are effective nevertheless because they provide simple explanations for otherwise irrational emotions, such as resentment or xenophobic fear in the face of perceived threats. The idea that President Obama is secretly a Muslim pretending to be a Christian in order to overthrow the U.S. government makes rational sense of the irrational feeling of threat many white people had upon his ascension to the presidency. That Muslims are trying to sneak Sharia law into Texas makes rational sense of the feeling of fear caused by a combination of religious nationalists spreading anti-Muslim xenophobia, and ISIS propaganda videos of terrorist acts committed on far-off shores. Once a public accepts the comfort of conspiracy thinking as an explanation for irrational fears and resentments, its members will cease to be guided by reason in political deliberation.

• • •

Spreading wild conspiracy theories benefits fascist movements. And yet how can this be, if reason always wins out in the public square of liberal democracy? Shouldn't liberal democracy promote a full airing of all possibilities, even false and bizarre ones, because the truth will eventually prevail in the marketplace of ideas?

Perhaps philosophy's most famous defense of the freedom of speech was articulated by John Stuart Mill, who defended the ideal in his 1859 work, *On Liberty*. In chapter 2, "Of the Liberty of Thought and Discussion," Mill sets out to establish that silencing any opinion is wrong, even if the opinion is false. To silence a false opinion is wrong, because knowledge arises only from the "collision [of truth] with error." In other words, true belief becomes knowledge only by emerging victorious from the din of argument and disagreement and discussion.

According to Mill, knowledge emerges only as the result of deliberation with opposing positions, which must occur either with actual opponents or through internal dialogue. Without this process, even true belief remains mere "prejudice." We must allow all speech, even defense of false claims and conspiracy theories, because it is only then that we have a chance of achieving knowledge.

Whether rightly or wrongly, many associate Mill's *On Liberty* with the motif of a "marketplace of ideas," a realm that, if left to operate on its own, will drive out prejudice and falsehood and produce knowledge. But the notion of a "marketplace of ideas," like that of a free market generally, is predicated on a utopian conception of consumers. In the case of the metaphor of the marketplace of ideas, the utopian assumption is that conversation works by exchange of reasons, with one party offering its reasons, which are then countered by the reasons of an opponent, until the truth ultimately emerges. But conversation is not just used to communicate information. Conversation is also used to shut out perspectives, raise fears, and heighten prejudice. The philosopher Ernst Cassirer writes in 1946, remarking on the changes wrought by fascist politics on the German language:

> If we study our modern political myths and the use that has been made of them we find in them, to our great surprise, not only a transvaluation of all our ethical values but also a transformation of human speech. . . . New words have been coined, and even the old ones are used in a new sense; they have undergone a deep change of meaning. This change of meaning depends upon the fact that these words which formerly were used in a descriptive, logical, or semantic sense are now used as magic words that are destined to produce certain effects and to stir up certain emotions. Our ordinary words are charged with meanings; but these new-fangled words are charged with feelings and violent passions.[2]

The argument for the "marketplace of ideas" presupposes that words are used only in their "descriptive, logical, or semantic sense." But in politics, and most vividly in fascist politics, language is not used simply, or even chiefly, to convey information but to elicit emotion.

The argument from the "marketplace of ideas" model for free speech works only if the underlying disposition of the society is to accept the force of reason over the power of irrational resentments and prejudice. If the society is divided, however, then a demagogic politician can exploit the division by using language to sow fear, accentuate prejudice, and call for revenge against members of hated groups. Attempting to counter such rhetoric with reason is akin to using a pamphlet against a pistol.

Mill seems to think that knowledge, and *only* knowledge, emerges from arguments between dedicated opponents. Such a process, according to Mill, destroys prejudice. Mill would surely then be pleased with the Russian television network RT, whose motto is "Question More." If Mill is correct, RT, which features voices from across the broadest possible political spectrum, from neo-Nazis to far leftists, should be the paradigm source of knowledge production. However, RT's strategy was not devised to produce knowledge. It was rather devised as a propaganda technique, to undermine trust in basic democratic institutions. Objective truth is drowned out in the resulting cacophony of voices. The effect of RT, as well as the myriad conspiracy-theory-producing websites across the world, including in the United States, has been to destabilize the kind of shared reality that is in fact required for democratic contestation.

What did Mill get wrong here?

Disagreement requires a shared set of presuppositions about the world. Even dueling requires agreement about the rules. You and I might disagree about whether President Obama's healthcare plan was good policy. But if you suspect that President Obama was an undercover Muslim spy seeking to destroy the United States, and I do not, our discussion will not be productive. We will not be talking about the costs and benefits of Obama's health policy, but rather about whether any of his policies mask a devious antidemocratic agenda.

In devising the strategy for RT, Russian propagandists, or "political technologists," realized that with a cacophony of opinions and outlandish possibilities, one could undermine the basic background set of presuppositions about the world that allows for productive inquiry. One can hardly have reasoned discussion about climate policy when one suspects that the scientists who tell us about climate change have a secret pro-homosexual agenda (as for example the evangelical media leader Tony Perkins suggested on an October 29, 2014, edition of his radio program *Washington Watch*[3]). Allowing every opinion into the public sphere and giving it serious time for consideration, far from resulting in a process that is conducive to knowledge formation via deliberation, destroys its very possibility. Responsible media in a liberal democracy must, in the face of this threat, try to report the truth, and resist the temptation to report on every possible theory, no matter how fantastical, as long as someone advances it.

• • •

What happens when conspiracy theories become the coin of politics, and mainstream media and educational institutions are discredited, is that citizens no longer have a common reality that can serve as background for democratic deliberation. In such a situation, citizens have no choice but to look for markers to follow other than truth or reliability. What happens in such cases, as we see across the world, is that citizens look to politics for tribal identifications, for addressing personal grievances, and for entertainment. When news becomes sports, the strongman achieves a certain measure of popularity. Fascist politics transforms the news from a conduit of information and reasoned debate into a spectacle with the strongman as the star.

Fascist politics, as we have seen, seeks to undermine trust in the press and universities. But the information sphere of a healthy democratic society does not include just democratic institutions. Spreading general suspicion and doubt undermines the bonds of mutual respect between fellow citizens, leaving them with deep wells of mistrust not just toward institutions but also toward one another. Fascist politics seeks to destroy the relations of mutual respect between citizens that are the foundation of a healthy liberal democracy, replacing them ultimately with trust in one figure alone, the leader. When fascist politics is at its most successful, the leader is regarded by the followers as singularly trustworthy.

In the 2016 U.S. presidential election, Donald Trump repeatedly and openly lied, and openly flouted long-sacrosanct liberal norms. The U.S. mainstream media dutifully reported his many lies. His opponent, Hillary Clinton, followed liberal norms of equal respect; her one violation of these norms, which occurred when she called some of the supporters of her opponent "deplorables," was endlessly thrown back in her face. And yet again and again, Americans found Trump to be the more authentic candidate. By giving voice to shocking sentiments that were presumed to be unsuitable for public discourse, Trump was taken to be *speaking his mind*. This is how, by exhibiting classic demagogic behavior, a politician can come to be seen as the more authentic candidate, even when he is manifestly dishonest.

The possibility of this kind of politics arises under certain conditions in a democracy.[4] In another kind of propagandistic twisted meaning, politicians can convey the message that they are the representative of the common good by explicitly attacking the common good. To see how this perplexing situation is possible, one can look at how in the U.S. political system these conditions have arisen in the recent past.

In Federalist Paper No. 10, James Madison argued that the United States had to take the form of a representative democracy and seek to elect leaders who best represented the values of democracy. An election campaign is supposed to present candidates seeking to show that they have the common interests of all citizens at heart. Two factors have eroded the protections that representative democracy is supposed to provide. First, candidates must raise huge sums to run for office (ever more so since the 2010 Citizens United decision by the U.S. Supreme Court). As a result, they represent the interests of their large donors. However, because it is a democracy, they must also try to make the case that they represent the common interest. They must pretend that the best interests of the multinational corporations that fund their campaigns are also the common interest.

Second, some voters do not share democratic values, and politicians must appeal to them as well. When large inequalities exist, the problem is aggravated. Some voters are simply more attracted to a system that favors their own particular religion, race, gender, or birth position. The resentment that flows from unmet expectations can be redirected against minority groups seen as not sharing dominant traditions; goods that go to them are represented by demagogic politicians, in a zero-sum way, as taking goods away from majority groups. Some voters see such groups, rather than the behavior of economic elites, as responsible for their unmet expectations. Candidates must attract these voters while appearing not to flout democratic values. As a result, many politicians use coded language to exploit resentment, as in the Republican Party's "Southern strategy," in order to avoid the charge of excluding the perspectives of opposing groups. As the infamous Republican political strategist Lee Atwater, then a consultant in Reagan's White House (later the campaign manager for George H. W. Bush's '88 win), explained that racist intent had to be made less overt over time in a 1981 interview with political scientist Alexander Lamis:

> By 1968 you can't say "nigger"—that hurts you, backfires. So you say stuff like, uh, forced busing, states' rights, and all that stuff, and you're getting so abstract. Now, you're talking about cutting taxes, and all these things you're talking about are totally economic things and a byproduct of them is, blacks get hurt worse than whites. . . .[5]

Tactics like these are not a secret, and for these reasons, U.S. politics has appeared insincere to many voters. And they are sick of it—they crave principled, honest politicians. They want politicians to *tell it like it is*. And they will seek such candidates even in the absence of a clear set of values they share.

But how can politicians signal that they are not hypocritical, especially when voters have grown accustomed to what seems, for both real and contrived reasons, to be a deep stratum of hypocrisy?

One way for candidates to address the widespread disgust with hypocrisy is to represent themselves as champions of democratic values. In a democratic culture, such candidates would theoretically be the most attractive. However, this is not a promising strategy in certain political climates. It is difficult to represent oneself as genuinely representing the common interest in an environment of general distrust. It does not appeal to voters who reject democratic values, such as racial or gender equality, or those who simply deny that inequalities exist. And there will be fierce competition for voters who support democratic values between candidates representing themselves as their champions.

But there is a way a politician could appear to be sincere without having to vie against other candidates pursuing the same strategy: by standing for division and conflict without apology. Such a candidate might openly side with Christians over Muslims and atheists, or native-born Americans over immigrants, or whites over blacks, or the rich over the poor. They might openly and brazenly lie. In short, one could signal authenticity by openly and explicitly rejecting what are presumed to be sacrosanct political values.

Such politicians would be a breath of fresh air in a political culture that seems dominated by real and imagined hypocrisy. They would be especially compelling if they demonstrated their supposed authenticity by explicitly targeting groups that are disliked by the voters they seek to attract. Such open rejection of democratic values would be taken as political bravery, as a signal of authenticity. It was not without justification that Plato saw in democracy's freedoms an allowance for the rise of a skilled demagogue who would take advantage of these freedoms to tear reality asunder, offering himself or herself as a substitute.

Ever since Plato and Aristotle wrote on the topic, political theorists have known that democracy cannot flourish on soil poisoned by inequality. It is not merely that the resentments bred by such divisions are tempting targets for a demagogue. The more important point is that dramatic inequality poses a mortal danger to the shared reality required for a healthy liberal democracy. Those who benefit from inequalities are often burdened by certain illusions that prevent them from recognizing the contingency of their privilege. When inequalities grow particularly stark, these illusions tend to metastasize. What dictator, king, or emperor has not suspected that he was chosen by the gods for his role? What colonial power has not entertained delusions of its ethnic superiority, or the superiority of its religion, culture, and way of life, superiority that supposedly justifies its imperial expansions and conquests? In the antebellum American South, whites believed that slavery was a great gift to those who were enslaved. The harshness of Southern planters to enslaved persons who sought to flee or rebel was in no small part due to their conviction that such behavior revealed lack of gratitude.

Extreme economic inequality is toxic to liberal democracy because it breeds delusions that mask reality, undermining the possibility of joint deliberation to solve society's divisions. Those who benefit from large inequalities are inclined to believe that they have earned their privilege, a delusion that prevents them from seeing reality as it is. Even those who demonstrably do not benefit from hierarchies can be made to believe that they do; hence the use of racism to ensnare poor white citizens in the United States into supporting tax cuts for extravagantly wealthy whites who happen to share their skin color.

Liberal equality means that those with different levels of power and wealth nevertheless are regarded as having equal worth. Liberal equality is, by definition, meant to be compatible with economic inequality. And yet, when economic inequality is sufficiently extreme, the myths that are required to sustain it are bound to threaten liberal equality as well.

The myths that arise under conditions of dramatic material inequality legitimize ignoring the proper common referee for public discourse, which is the world. To completely destroy reality, fascist politics replaces the liberal ideal of equality with its opposite: hierarchy.

5

HIERARCHY

The fates of human beings are not equal. Men differ in their states of health and wealth or social status or what not. Simple observation shows that in every such situation he who is more favored feels the never ceasing need to look upon his position as in some way "legitimate," upon his advantage being "deserved," and the other's disadvantage being brought about by the latter's "fault." That the purely accidental causes of the difference may be ever so obvious makes no difference.

—Max Weber, *On Law in Economy and Society* (1967), 335

The history of liberal citizenship—of equality under the law—has generally been one of expansion, gradually encompassing people of all races, religions, and genders, to name a few examples. This is true, too, of political philosophy. Influenced, for example, by theorists of disability, philosophers have expanded the notion of human dignity to include those who cannot under most circumstances employ their capacity for political judgment. In the twenty-first century, most liberal thinkers have included a generous recognition of universal human status and dignity to include the ability to feel physical suffering, feel emotions, and express identity and empathy in multiple ways.

According to fascist ideology, by contrast, nature imposes hierarchies of power and dominance that are flatly inconsistent with the equality of respect presupposed by liberal democratic theory.

Hierarchy is a kind of mass delusion, one readily exploited by fascist politics. A major branch of social psychology, Social Dominance Theory, pioneered by Jim Sidanius and Felicia Pratto, studies these delusions under the name of "legitimation myths."[1] The opening passages of a 2006 literature review of the previous fifteen years of Social Dominance Theory include the claim:

> Regardless of a society's form of government, the contents of its fundamental belief system, or the complexity of its social and economic arrangements, human societies tend to organise as group-based social hierarchies in which at least one group enjoys greater social status and power than other groups.[2]

Fascist ideology, then, takes advantage of a human tendency to organize society hierarchically, and fascist politicians represent the myths that legitimize their hierarchies as immutable facts. Their principle justification of hierarchy is nature itself. For the fascist, the principle of equality is a denial of natural law, which sets certain traditions, those of the more powerful, over others. The natural law allegedly places men over women, and members of the chosen nation of the fascist over other groupings.

Nature is repeatedly invoked in fascist writing. On March 21, 1861, Alexander H. Stephens, the vice president of the Confederacy, delivered an address that has come to be known as the Cornerstone Speech. In it, he denounces the principles of liberty and equality enshrined in the U.S. Constitution as violations of the laws of nature:

> Our new government is founded upon exactly the opposite idea [of equality]; its foundations are laid, its corner-stone rests, upon the great truth that the negro is not equal to the white man; that slavery subordination to the superior race is his natural and normal condition.[3]

The Cornerstone Speech makes vivid the characteristically fascist logic that liberal democratic principles are in conflict with nature and must therefore be abandoned:

> I recollect of once having heard a gentleman from one of the northern States, of great power and ability, announce in the House of Representatives, with imposing effect, that we of the South would be compelled, ultimately, to yield upon this subject of slavery, that it was as impossible to war successfully against a principle in politics, as it was in physics or mechanics. That the principle would ultimately prevail. That we, in maintaining slavery as it exists with us, were warring against a principle, a principle founded in nature, the principle of the equality of men. The reply I made to him was, that upon his own grounds, we should, ultimately, succeed, and that he and his associates, in this crusade against our institutions, would ultimately fail. The truth announced, that it was as impossible to war successfully against a principle in politics as it was in physics and mechanics, I admitted; but told him that it was he, and those acting with him, who were warring against a principle. They were attempting to make things equal which the Creator had made unequal.

The Confederacy, Stephens declares, is "founded upon principles in strict conformity" with the laws of nature, which are "the real 'corner-stone' in our new edifice." Stephens denounces those who would deny the inequality of racial inferiority as "fanatics" who reject "the eternal principles of truth." The Confederacy, like Hitler's

Reich, was built to defend "the aristocratic principle in nature," the principle of racial hierarchy.

In the university, there remain powerful voices who call for "reasoned discourse" about genetic differences between races in such aspects as intelligence or propensity to violence, and in them we find a clear echo of Stephens's condemnation of abolitionists as irrational "fanatics" for their firm belief in racial equality. In his March 2018 article for *The Guardian,* "The Unwelcome Revival of Race Science," Gavin Evans describes how "race science is [leaching] into mainstream discourse" via figures such as the political scientist Charles Murray and the Harvard psychologist Steven Pinker. According to Evans, in 2005, Pinker began popularizing the view that "Ashkenazi Jews are innately particularly intelligent," a view that Evans describes as "the smiling face of race science"; the claim that Ashkenazi Jews are innately particularly intelligent invites the reader to draw conclusions about other groups and their "innate intelligence." In a 2007 piece for the online venue The Edge, Pinker decries how "political correctness" has prevented researchers from studying "dangerous ideas," including "Do women, on average, have a different profile of aptitudes and emotions than men?" and "Are Ashkenazi Jews, on average, smarter than gentiles because their ancestors were selected for the shrewdness needed in money lending?" and "Do African American men have higher levels of testosterone, on average, than white men?" The concern about this kind of writing is that it presents those who seek a natural source for inequality as brave truth-seekers, driven by reason to reject the heart's plea for equality. This research has proven to be suspect, at best. And yet, the search for the natural source of inequality that Stephens pointed to as fact somehow continues, grail-like.

Fascists argue that natural hierarchies of worth in fact exist, and that their existence undermines the obligation for equal consideration. One sees a valuation of this kind in the words of the many white supporters of Donald Trump in the 2016 U.S. presidential election who regularly spoke of their disdain for supposedly "undeserving" recipients of U.S. governmental largesse in the form of healthcare, by which they often meant their black fellow citizens. In his run for the presidency, Trump exploited the lengthy history of ranking Americans into a hierarchy of worth by race, the "deserving" versus the "undeserving."

When pressed by journalists to justify a distinction between the "deserving" and the "undeserving," Americans who use such vocabulary reach in the first instance for the language of "hardworking" versus "lazy" rather than for the language of racial distinction. But this hardly justifies the division of fellow citizens into such categories. First, in the United States, racism has often taken the form of associating blackness with laziness. Such language has always been a code for division by racial hierarchy. Second, it betrays confusion about the concept of liberal democracy to measure worthiness by a supposed capacity for hard work. It is no part of liberal democratic theory that basic equal respect is won by hard work. The idea behind liberal democracy is that *all* of us are equally deserving of the basic goods of society.

Some would argue for the existence of inherent differences between groups of people along lines of intelligence and self-control, and still claim to value equal dignity for all. Nevertheless, history gives us salient examples of the difficulty of believing in systematic group differences while upholding the equal treatment of others. In his 1920 essay "Of the Ruling of Men," W.E.B. Du Bois writes about the failure to give women equal voice in the determination of policy:

> . . . women have been excluded from modern democracy because of the persistent theory of female subjection and because it was argued that their husbands or other male folks would look to their interests. Now, manifestly, most husbands, fathers, and brothers, will, so far as they know how or as they realize women's needs, look after them. . . . We have but to view the unsatisfactory relations of the sexes the world over and the problem of children to realize how desperately we need this excluded wisdom.[4]

Such examples suggest the difficulty of maintaining an ethic of equal worth in the presence of a belief in genetic group differences in cognitive abilities or the capacity to control one's own actions. No one is forced by a confrontation with reality into believing in these kinds of hierarchal differences between, for example, genders, or racial or ethnic groups. There is no persuasive evidence for such hierarchies, despite centuries of attempts to establish them by religious edict or scientific investigation. Those who strenuously argue for racial hierarchies of intelligence or the capacity for self-control, while denying any interest in illiberal moral or political consequences, tend to be misguided.

• • •

Establishing hierarchies of worth is of course a means of obtaining and retaining power—a kind of power that liberal democracy attempts to delegitimize. On this point, there are critiques of liberal ideals from both the traditional left and the traditional right. Leftist critiques of liberalism point out its supposed failure to account for structural, historical inequalities, in that the practice of liberalism does not typically include remedies for past injustice. Leftist critics of liberalism also argue that the liberal ideals of equality and freedom can be used to entrench the power of dominant groups. For example, it can be argued that ways to remedy entrenched structural injustice—say, affirmative action programs—violate liberal ideals of equal treatment. Critiques of liberalism from the right have a different flavor. Right-wing critics warn that liberal equality can be used by marginalized groups as a weapon to displace the privileged status of dominant groups and their traditions.

Both left-wing and right-wing critiques of liberalism focus on the fact that liberal ideals ignore differences in power. Leftist critics argue that by doing so, liberal ideals entrench preexisting inequalities. Rightist critics argue that by ignoring differences in power, liberalism makes dominant groups susceptible to having their privileged status overturned by forced, and therefore unjust, "power sharing." We find the latter critique of liberalism explicit in Hitler's writings as well as *The Protocols of the Elders of Zion.*

The Protocols, recall, is a forgery that is written like an instruction manual by "the elders of Zion," supposed leaders among Jews, to other Jews, to take over and dominate the world on behalf of the Jewish people. It begins by instructing the reader to "infect the opponent with the idea of freedom, so-called liberalism." According to *The Protocols,* liberalism weakens the "opponent" (here, the Christian), by drawing Christians into recognizing the equal rights of Jews. If Christians accept liberalism, they will be led to give equal respect and equal recognition to other religious groups, thereby ceding their dominant traditional position:

> Political freedom is an idea but not a fact. This idea one must know how to apply whenever it appears necessary with this bait of an idea to attract the masses of the people to one's party for the purpose of crushing another who is in authority. This task is rendered easier if the opponent has himself been infected with the idea of freedom, SO-CALLED LIBERALISM, and, for the sake of an idea, is willing to yield some of his power. It is precisely here that the triumph of our theory appears; the slackened reins of government are immediately, by the law of life, caught up and gathered together by a new hand, because the blind might of the nation cannot for one single day exist without guidance, and the new authority merely fits into the place of the old already weakened by liberalism.

In the statement "Political freedom is an idea, but not a fact," the purported authors of *The Protocols* echo the theme of Stephens's Cornerstone Speech—that political freedom, and hence political equality, is an illusion, an impossibility, given that nature requires one group to lead and dominate. *The Protocols* suggests spreading the myth of "political freedom," or "liberalism," to members of dominant groups. By accepting the myth of "political freedom," those in power will grant equal status to those who lack it. But since "the law of life," that is, nature, demands that one group rule, once Jews are granted some of the power by the dominant Christians, they can then seize all of the power from them.

Equality, according to the fascist, is the Trojan horse of liberalism. The part of Odysseus can be variously played—by Jews, by homosexuals, by Muslims, by non-whites, by feminists, etc. Anyone spreading the doctrine of liberal equality is either a dupe, "infected by the idea of freedom," or an enemy of the nation who is spreading the ideals of liberalism only with devious and indeed illiberal aims.

The fascist project combines anxiety about loss of status for members of the true "nation," with fear of equal recognition of hated minority groups. For the twentieth-century Ku Klux Klan, Jews were often perceived as the force behind black racial equality: Jews sought to advance black equality in order to dilute pure white blood and undermine the white Christian ethnostate. As the Nazi ideologue Alfred Rosenberg writes in a 1923 commentary on *The Protocols of the Elders of Zion,* "it is well known that Jews of all kinds pretend to fight for freedom and peace day after day; their speakers drip with humanity and love of mankind, as long as Jewish interests are thereby promoted."[5] In Nazi ideology, Jews operate with the same hierarchal views of nature as Nazis do but use the universal principles of liberal democracy as a façade to advance it. It is classic fascist politics, as we have seen, to represent the actual defenders of liberal democracy as defending its ideals only in the service of undermining them.

According to fascists, liberals and Marxists (or "cultural Marxists") advance the ideals of equality and liberty, spreading their ideas as "infections" to members of the dominant group which leads them to willingly hand over their power. In the case of women's equality, acceptance of liberal ideals leads to the destruction of the virtuous patriarchal society that is the basis of fascist myth. Lindbergh's America First movement repudiated liberal ideals as leading to the pollution of the "pure blood" of the white nation via immigration. In the case of contemporary Russia, and much of the U.S. Christian right, liberal democracy leads to the legitimation of immigration and the supposed introduction of mass rape by immigrants, and to the acceptance of homosexuality together with its supposedly attendant sin of "degeneracy."

• • •

Hierarchy benefits fascist politics in another way: Those who are accustomed to its benefits can be easily led to view liberal equality as a source of victimization. Those who benefit from hierarchy will adopt a myth of their own superiority, which will occlude basic facts about social reality. They will distrust pleas for tolerance and inclusion made by liberals on the grounds that these pleas are masks for power grabs by other groups. Fascist politics feeds off the sense of aggrieved victimization caused by loss of hierarchal status.

Empires in decline are particularly susceptible to fascist politics because of this sense of loss. It is in the very nature of empire to create a hierarchy; empires legitimize their colonial enterprises by a myth of their own exceptionalism. In the course of decline, the population is easily led to a sense of national humiliation that can be mobilized in fascist politics to serve various purposes. During the late nineteenth and early twentieth centuries, the Ottoman Empire experienced a tremendous collapse, losing more than 400,000 square miles of territory in Africa and Europe, including Libya, Albania, Macedonia, Bosnia, Herzegovina, and Crete. The Ottoman sultanate was overthrown in 1908, and in 1913 the empire was taken over by extremist ultranationalists who preached a vision of a completely mythic pure ethnic Turkish past that was placed in threat by the presence of non-Turkish, non-Muslim minorities (the mythology here is particularly extreme, as the Ottoman Empire's home of modern-day Turkey was the site of one of the world's most powerful and longest-lasting Christian empires, Byzantium). They were able to exploit the sense of humiliation and resentment and loss of territory to bring about, in the second decade of the twentieth century, one of the more horrific crimes in history, the massacre of the Armenian Christian population of Turkey.

In "Why Now? It's the Empire, Stupid," a June 2016 article in *The Nation,* the NYU historian Greg Grandin argues that Donald Trump's politics is effective in the context of the 2016 campaign because it comes at a time of decline for the American empire. We are witnessing the passing of the era after the end of the Cold War in which the United States reigned supreme in the world as the only remaining superpower. In the article, he argues that an empire gives rise among its citizens to a comforting myth of superiority, thereby concealing the various social and structural problems that otherwise would lead to political difficulties. With its demise, the citizens of a once powerful empire must confront the fact that their exceptionalism was a myth. Grandin writes that beginning in 2008—about when Barack Obama won the presidential election—"the safety valve of empire closed, gummed up by the catastrophic war in Iraq combined with the 2008 financial crisis. . . . Because Obama came to power in the ruins of neoliberalism and neoconservatism, empire [was] no longer able to dilute the passions, satisfy the interests, and unify the divisions."

When imperial hierarchy collapses and social reality is laid bare, hierarchical sentiment in the home country tends to arise as a mechanism to preserve the familiar and comforting illusion of superiority. Fascist politics thrives off the resulting sense of aggrieved loss and victimization that results from the ever more tenuous and difficult struggle to defend a sense of cultural, ethnic, religious, gendered, or national superiority.

6

VICTIMHOOD

In fascist politics, the opposing notions of equality and discrimination get mixed up with each other. The Civil Rights Act of 1866 made the newly emancipated black Americans of the South into U.S. citizens and protected their civil rights. It was passed by the Senate and the House on March 14, 1866. Later that month, President Andrew Johnson vetoed the Civil Rights Act, on the grounds that "this law establishes for the security of the colored race safeguards which go infinitely beyond any that the General Government have ever provided for the white race." As W.E.B. Du Bois notes, Johnson perceived minimal safeguards at the start of a path toward future black equality as "discrimination against the white race."[1]

Today, white Americans wildly overestimate the extent of U.S. progress toward racial equality over the past fifty years. Economic inequality between black and white Americans is roughly at the point it was during Reconstruction; for every $100 the average white family has accumulated, the average black family has just $5; and yet, as Jennifer Richeson, Michael Kraus, and Julian Rucker have shown in their 2017 paper, "Americans Misperceive Racial Economic Equality," white American citizens are widely ignorant of this fact, believing that racial economic inequality has dramatically narrowed.[2] Forty-five percent of President Donald Trump's supporters believe that whites are the most discriminated-against racial group in America; 54 percent of Trump's supporters believe that Christians are the most persecuted religious group in America. There is a crucial distinction, of course, between feelings of resentment and oppression and genuine inequality and discrimination.

There is a long history of social psychological research about the fact that increased representation of members of traditional minority groups is experienced by dominant groups as threatening in various ways.[3] More recently, a growing body of social psychological evidence substantiates the phenomenon of dominant group feelings of victimization at the prospect of sharing power equally with members of minority groups. A great deal of recent attention has been paid in the United States to the fact that around 2050, the United States will become a "majority-minority" country, meaning that whites will no longer be a majority of Americans. Taking advantage of the salience of this information, some social psychologists have tested what happens when white Americans are primed with it.

In a 2014 study, the psychologists Maureen Craig and Jennifer Richeson found that simply making salient the impending national shift to a "majority-minority" country significantly increased politically unaffiliated white Americans' support for right-wing policies.[4] For example, reading about an impending racial shift of the country from majority white to majority nonwhite made white American subjects less inclined to support affirmative action, more inclined to support restrictions on immigration, and, perhaps surprisingly, more likely to support "race neutral" conservative policies such as increasing defense spending. Summarizing this research in a forthcoming review article, Maureen Craig, Julian Rucker, and Jennifer Richeson write, "this growing body of work finds clear evidence that White Americans (i.e., the current racial majority) experience the impending 'majority-minority' shift as a threat to their dominant (social, economic, political, and cultural) status."[5] This feeling of threat can be marshaled politically as support for right-wing movements. This dialectic is far from native to the United States; it is rather a general feature of group psychology. The exploitation of the feeling of victimization by dominant groups at the prospect of sharing citizenship and power with minorities is a universal element of contemporary international fascist politics.

. . .

In the face of discrimination, oppressed groups throughout history have risen up in movements that proclaimed pride for their endangered identities. In Western Europe, the Jewish nationalism of the Zionist movement arose as a response to toxic anti-Semitism. In the United States, black nationalism arose as a response to toxic racism. In their origins, these nationalist movements were *responses* to oppression. Anticolonialist struggles typically take place under the banner of nationalism; for example, Mahatma Gandhi employed Indian nationalism as a tool against British rule. This kind of nationalism, the nationalism that arises from oppression, is not fascist in origin. These forms of nationalism, in their original formations, are equality-driven nationalist movements.

In colonialism, the imperial nation typically presents itself as the bearer of universal ideals. For example, British colonialists in Kenya presented Christianity as the universal ideal and the many local tribal religions as primitive and savage. In part a response to this religious oppression, the Mau Mau rebellion against Britain valorized the traditional Gikuyu religion—Mau Mau rebels took an oath to Ngai, the Gikuyu god. The Mau Mau colonialist struggle used nationalist religious ideals to fight colonialism. But the goal of the Mau Mau struggle was not to fight for the *superiority* of the Gikuyu religious traditions over the British religious traditions. The goal was rather to fight for the *equality* of the Gikuyu traditions against the British demonization of them as forms of primitive savagery. To do so, it was necessary to elevate these traditions, to hold them as sacrosanct and special, not as a means of repudiating the value of British traditions, but rather as a means to emphasize a demand for equal respect. This kind of nationalism is therefore in no sense *opposed* to equality; instead, despite appearances to the contrary, equality is its *goal*.

The case is similar with the Black Lives Matter movement in the United States today. Its opponents try to represent the slogan as the illiberal nationalist claim that *only* black lives matter. But the slogan is hardly intended as a repudiation of the value of white lives in the United States. Rather, it intends to point out that in the United States, white lives have been taken to matter more than other lives. The point of the slogan Black Lives Matter is to call attention to a failure of equal respect. In its context, it means, "Black lives matter *too*."

At the core of fascism is loyalty to tribe, ethnic identity, religion, tradition, or, in a word, *nation*. But, in stark contrast to a version of nationalism with equality as its goal, fascist nationalism is a repudiation of the liberal democratic ideal; it is nationalism in the service of domination, with the goal of preserving, maintaining, or gaining a position at the top of a hierarchy of power and status.

. . .

The difference between the nationalism motivated by oppression and nationalism for the sake of domination is clear when one reflects upon their respective relationships with equality. But that difference can be invisible from the inside. Whether or not the anguish that accompanies loss of privileged status is similar to the sense of oppression that accompanies genuine marginalization, it is anguish nevertheless. If I grew up in a country in which my religious holidays were the national holidays, it would feel like marginalization to have my children grow up in a more egalitarian country in which their religious holidays and traditions are just one of many. If I grew up in a society in which every character in the movies I see and the television programs I watch looked like me, it would feel like marginalization to see the occasional protagonist who does not. I would start to feel that my culture is no longer "for me." If I grew up seeing men as heroes and women as passive objects who worship them, it would feel like oppression to be robbed of my felt birthright by having to regard women as equals in the workplace or on the battlefield. Rectifying unjust inequalities will always bring pain to those who benefited from such injustices. This pain will inevitably be experienced by some as oppression.

. . .

Fascist propaganda typically features aching hymns to the sense of anguish that accompanies loss of dominant status. This sense of loss, which is genuine, is manipulated in fascist politics into aggrieved victimhood and exploited to justify past, continuing, or new forms of oppression.

For a white working-class male who is no longer employed, for structural economic reasons, to be told to "check your privilege" may increase the likelihood that he might see a level playing field in the agenda of white supremacy. Fascist politics makes great sport of such earnest liberal injunctions. Inquiry into structural inequality requires collective public reflection on the strong evidence that reveals how race and gender-based status has given white males, and to a lesser degree white females, degrees of freedom never fully available to black citizens. "Check your privilege" is a call to whites to recognize the insulated social reality they navigate daily. However, the phrase is flung back into the public sphere as hypocrisy on the part of liberal elites, because white nationalist propaganda finds no racism against black citizens in 2017 America, but much against whites.

Fascist politics covers up structural inequality by attempting to invert, misrepresent, and subvert the long, hard effort to address it. Affirmative action at its best was designed to recognize and address structural inequality. But by falsely presenting affirmative action as uncoupled from individual merit, some of its detractors recast advocates of affirmative action as pursuing their own race- or gender-based "nationalism" to the detriment of hardworking white Americans, regardless of evidence. The experience of losing a once unquestioned, settled dignity—the dignity that comes with being white, not black—is easily captured by a language of white victimization.

The Men's Rights Activist (MRA) movement in the United States in the 1990s crystallized the loss of privilege experienced as victimization. In his 2013 book, *Angry White Men: American Masculinity at the End of an Era,* the Stony Brook sociologist Michael Kimmel writes:

> When white men are cast as the oppressors, normal, everyday middle-class white guys don't often feel all that power trickling down to them. . . . To the MRAs, the real victims in American society are men, and so they built organizations around men's anxieties and anger at feminism, groups like the Coalition for Free Men, the National Congress for Men, Men Achieving Liberty and Equality (MALE), and Men's Rights Inc. (MR, Inc.). These groups proclaim their commitment to equality and to ending sexism—which was why they were compelled to fight against feminism.[6]

Kimmel notes "a curious characteristic of these new legions of angry white men: although white men still have most of the power and control in the world, these particular white men feel like victims." He connects this sense of victimhood to the perpetuation of a mythic patriarchal past:

> These ideas also reflect a somewhat nostalgic longing for that past world, when men believed they could simply take their places among the nation's elite, simply by working hard and applying themselves. Alas, such a world never existed; economic elites have always managed to reproduce themselves despite the ideals of a meritocracy. But that hasn't stopped men from believing it. It is the American Dream. And when men fail, they are humiliated, with nowhere to place their anger.[7]

Promulgating a mythical hierarchal past works to create unreasonable expectations. When these expectations are not met, it feels like victimhood.[8]

Those who employ fascist political tactics deliberately take advantage of this emotion, manufacturing a sense of aggrieved victimization among the majority population, directing it at a group that is not responsible for it and promising to alleviate the feeling of victimization by punishing that group. In her book *Down Girl,* Kate Manne illustrates this by drawing a distinction between patriarchy and misogyny. Patriarchy, according to Manne, is the hierarchal ideology that engenders the unreasonable expectations of high status. Misogyny is what faces women who are blamed when patriarchal expectations are left unfulfilled. The logic of fascist politics has a vivid model in Manne's logic of misogyny.

Breitbart News is a powerful far-right U.S. media outlet filled with anti-immigrant propaganda representing refugees as public health threats, threats to civilization, and threats to law and order. In such outlets, we find clear expression of the way in which an aggrieved sense of victimization of dominant majorities can be weaponized for potential political gain. *Breitbart* has run dozens of articles with headlines related to Somali refugees in the United States, including those with titles such as "296 Refugees Diagnosed with Active TB in Minnesota, Ten Times Any Other State; Majority Are Somalis," and "Somalis: Least Educated of Refugees Arriving to U.S. in FY 2017." *Breitbart* was only a part of a wave of such propaganda in the United States around this time. In a video viewed three million times since it was posted in April 2015, Ann Corcoran of the far-right anti-immigrant group Refugee Resettlement Watch speaks of a plan of "Muslim colonization" of the United States, aided and abetted by international organizations such as the United Nations, federal agencies such as the U.S. State Department, and "Christian and Jewish groups assigned to seed them throughout the country." These outlets spread a sense of paranoia at a "fifth column" of "liberal" groups in our midst using the vocabulary of human rights to undermine the nation's traditions. But in doing so, they not only undermine liberal ideals, but also suggest that their targets should be subject to intense scrutiny or punishment merely on the basis that the dominant group feels fearful.

· · ·

Understanding the dynamics of power in a society is crucial to assessing claims of victimhood. Equality-driven nationalism can rapidly turn oppressive itself, if one is not paying enough attention to shifts in power. Some problematic nationalist sentiments arise from perfectly genuine histories of oppression. Serbians have unquestionably been oppressed in the past. And one does not have to go back to the Battle of Kosovo in 1389, from which Serbians draw a great deal of national anger and identity, to encounter such oppression; World War II will suffice, when Serbians were murdered en masse in concentration camps. Contemporary Serbians come from families who are able to summon up a legacy of persecution. Serbian nationalists used this background to justify the persecution of less powerful and more marginalized local Muslim populations.

In 1986, the Serbian Academy of Arts and Sciences

published a memorandum that is generally regarded as having set out the tenets of the toxic Serbian nationalism that led to so much subsequent bloodshed in the former Yugoslavia. The document serves as a useful guide to the connection between victimization and oppressive nationalist sentiment. At the time, the majority of the residents in the province of Kosovo, who were ethnically Albanian, were requesting greater autonomy. The document's authors describe the Albanian treatment of ethnic Serbs in Kosovo as a "physical, political, legal, and cultural genocide of the Serbian population." They declare, "No other Yugoslav nation has had its cultural and spiritual integrity so brutally trampled upon as the Serbian nation. No one else's literary and artistic heritage has been so despoiled and ravaged as the Serbian heritage." They speak of "consistent economic discrimination" against Serbia, and unyielding "economic subordination." They declare that the "vindictive policy toward this republic has not lost any of its edge with the passing of time. On the contrary, encouraged by its own success, it has grown ever stronger, to the point of genocide." The document uses a dramatically exaggerated narrative of Serbian victimization to call for a recommitment to the defense of ethnic Serbs, as well as to Serbia's traditional history and culture.

Slobodan Milošević was the president of Serbia from 1989 until 1997. On June 28, 1989, Milošević delivered a speech to a vast crowd gathered on the battlefield of the

Battle of Kosovo, at the celebration of its six hundredth anniversary. Milošević blamed the Serbian defeat at the hands of the Ottomans at the Battle of Kosovo, as well as "the fate Serbia suffered for a full six centuries," on a lack of Serbian unity—that is, a failure of Serbian nationalist spirit. In Milošević's speech, he said that the failure of Serbians to have nationalist pride had led over the centuries to "humiliation" and "agony" exceeding the cost of the fascist reign of terror during which several hundred thousand Serbians were killed. According to Milošević, the only way to end the centuries of horror was to embrace national unity—in other words, a Serbian nationalist agenda. The narrative of Serbian victimization led him to political victory. It also justified a series of brutal wars, including in Kosovo, after which Milošević was charged with genocide and crimes against humanity by the International Criminal Tribunal for actions taken against the Albanian population of Kosovo. There is no question that Serbians have, in the past, been oppressed by multiple forces. It hardly mattered that many of the groups Milošević would target were not actually responsible for any oppression of Serbians. Serbia's recent history under demagogic nationalists shows how a history of past oppression can be marshaled in fascist politics for military mobilization against phantom enemies.

Victimhood is an overwhelming emotion that also conceals the contradiction between equality-driven and domination-driven nationalist movements. When groups in power use the mask of nationalism of the oppressed, or of genuine oppression in the past, to advance their own hegemony, they are using it to undermine equality. When the Israeli right uses the unquestioned history of Jewish oppression to assert Jewish dominance over Palestinian lands and lives, they are relying on the sense of victimization to obscure the contradiction between a struggle for equal respect and a struggle for dominance. Oppression is a powerful motivation for action, but the questions of who is wielding it when, under what context and against whom, remain eternally crucial.

. . .

Nationalism is at the core of fascism. The fascist leader employs a sense of collective victimhood to create a sense of group identity that is by its nature opposed to the cosmopolitan ethos and individualism of liberal democracy. The group identity can be variously based—on skin color, on religion, on tradition, on ethnic origin. But it is always contrasted with a perceived other against whom the nation is to be defined. Fascist nationalism creates a dangerous "them" to guard against, at times to battle with, to control, in order to restore group dignity.

On October 12, 2017, Hungarian prime minister Viktor Orbán gave a speech at the International Consultation on Christian Persecution in Budapest. He begins by speaking of the "undoubtedly unfair" persecution of Christians in Europe, which he labels as "discriminatory" and "painful." After extolling Hungary's traditional role as defenders of Christian Europe, he declares that "today it is a fact that Christianity is the world's most persecuted religion," which according to him places "the future of the European way of life, and of our identity" into peril. According to him, "the greatest danger we [Europeans] face today is the indifferent, apathetic silence of a Europe which denies its Christian roots." The manifestation of this potentially catastrophic indifference to Europe's Christian roots is generous European immigration policies: "A group of Europe's intellectual and political leaders wishes to create a mixed society in Europe which, within just a few generations, will utterly transform the cultural and ethnic composition of our continent—and consequently its Christian identity."

In Orbán's speech, we have all the elements of the victimology of fascist politics. Orbán whips up irrational fear of immigrants, using Hungary's mythic past as the supposed defender of European Christianity to present himself as the warrior-leader who is brave enough to defend Christian Europe, which has been imperiled by the liberal elites ("Europe's intellectual and political leaders") who would let "the most persecuted religion in the world" be undermined from within by letting in a wave of immigrants. The refugees from brutal foreign wars are, in his eyes, a powerful invading force who seek to establish a "fifth column" inside Christian Europe's walls. Orbán asks his audience to repudiate "human rights" (ignoring their own home in Christianity) and other outdated concepts. As victims of persecution, he urges his audience to stand behind him as he returns Hungary to its glorious past as the mythic defender of Christian Europe against the barbarian, lawless hordes.

7

LAW AND ORDER

In 1989, five black teenagers—the "Central Park Five"—were arrested for the gang rape of a white woman jogger in New York City's Central Park. Newspapers at the time were filled with breathless accounts of "wilding" black lawless teens rampaging and raping white women. At the time, Donald Trump took out full-page ads in several New York City newspapers, describing them as "crazed misfits" and calling for their execution. Subsequently, it emerged not only that the Central Park Five were innocent, but that they were known to be innocent to many of those involved in their prosecution. Years later, all five were completely exonerated and given a cash settlement by the City of New York.

In November 2016, Jeff Sessions, now the U.S. attorney general, praised then president-elect Donald Trump's 1989 comments about the Central Park Five as demonstrating his commitment to "law and order." This is a striking understanding of law and order, not only because the teenagers were, in fact, completely innocent, but because Trump's words left no room for due process in the case. Norms of law and order in a liberal democratic state are fundamentally fair. Sessions's use of the phrase "law and order" instead seems to refer to a system of laws that declares young black men to be, in their very *existence,* violations of law and order.

. . .

A healthy democratic state is governed by laws that treat all citizens equally and justly, supported by bonds of mutual respect between people, including those tasked with policing them. Fascist law-and-order rhetoric is explicitly meant to divide citizens into two classes: those of the chosen nation, who are lawful by nature, and those who are not, who are inherently lawless. In fascist politics, women who do not fit traditional gender roles, nonwhites, homosexuals, immigrants, "decadent cosmopolitans," those who do not have the dominant religion, are in their very existence violations of law and order. By describing black Americans as a threat to law and order, demagogues in the United States have been able to create a strong sense of white national identity that requires protection from the nonwhite "threat." A similar tactic is used internationally now to create friend-enemy distinctions based on fear in order to unify populations against immigrants.

. . .

The history of National Socialism is a textbook example of fascist political national identity formation. Beginning in the 1880s, a version of ethnic nationalism developed in Austria and Germany that provided the wellspring from which the National Socialist movement flowed. The *völkisch* movement was rooted in a romanticized notion of ethnic purity of the German *Volk*. Anti-Semitism functioned within *völkisch* thought as part of the definition of the German *Volk*; the *Volk* were defined by contrast with their enemy, the Jews. The National Socialists also used what surely must be the most common method of sowing fear about a minority group—painting them as threats to law and order.

In the spring of 1936, my grandmother, Ilse Stanley, had just returned from a theater tour that had kept her away from Berlin for almost the whole winter, only to discover a city in which "more and more friends were missing." Soon after her return, a cousin arrived at her home. The Gestapo, her cousin told her, had taken her husband away to a concentration camp. In her 1957 memoir, *The Unforgotten,* my grandmother describes asking her cousin about the reasons for her husband's arrest. Her answer:

> Because he was a criminal with a record. He had paid two fines in court: one for speeding and one for some other traffic fine. They said they finally wanted to do what the court had missed doing all these years: to get rid of all Jews with criminal records. A traffic fine— a criminal record!

The first half of my grandmother's book is a careful accounting of the years following Hitler's rise to power. In it, she documents how difficult it was to get the German Jewish community to understand the peril they faced. She understood this peril from the inside as a result of her work rescuing prisoners from the concentration camp at Sachsenhausen while disguised as a Nazi social worker. Because of what she witnessed in the camp, she was aware, as many of her fellow Jews were not, of the full horror of what was occurring, which was, as with refugee and immigrant detention centers in the United States right now, kept hidden from the general population. She repeatedly writes of her difficulty in persuading friends and family members to leave. After all, most German Jews did not think of themselves as criminals.

In February 2016, the far-right SVP (the Schweizerische Volkspartei) introduced a referendum in Switzerland to expel "immigrants," including even second- or third-generation Swiss-born residents found guilty of as little as a few parking violations. The referendum seemed sure to pass. It was partly because of the efforts of Operation Libero, a group founded by Swiss students who organized to change the narrative of deporting "criminal immigrants," that the referendum was defeated.

In the United States, Donald Trump rode to the presidency with a call to expel "criminal aliens." Since he has taken office, he has continued targeting immigrants. Both he and his administration regularly stoke fear of immigrants by connecting them to criminality. Again and again, we are presented with the specter of "criminal aliens"—and not just in remarks but also in official documents, such as the announcement of a new office in the Department of Homeland Security devoted to helping "victims of crimes committed by criminal aliens."

The word "criminal" has a literal meaning, of course, but it also has a resonant meaning—people who by their nature are insensitive to society's norms, drawn to violate the law by self-interest or malice. We do not generally use the term to describe those who may have inadvertently broken a law or who may have been compelled to violate a law in a desperate circumstance. Someone who runs to catch a bus is not thereby a runner; someone who commits a crime is not thereby a criminal. The word "criminal" attributes a certain type of *character* to someone.

Psychologists have studied a practice they call linguistic intergroup bias. It turns out we tend to describe the actions of those we regard as one of "us" quite differently than we describe the actions of those we regard as one of "them."

If someone we regard as one of "us" does something bad—for example, steals a chocolate bar—we tend to describe the action concretely. In other words, if my friend Daniel steals a chocolate bar, I will tend to characterize what he did as "stealing a chocolate bar." On the other hand, if someone we regard as one of "them" does the same thing, we tend to describe the action more abstractly, by imputing bad character traits to the person committing it. If Jerome, who is regarded as one of "them," steals a chocolate bar, he is much more likely to be described as a thief or a criminal. If a white American sees a well-dressed white American handcuffed in the back of a police car, the question that comes to mind might be what happened that led to that particular arrest. If a white American sees a black American handcuffed in the back of a police car, the question that presents itself might instead be how the police got "that criminal."

The reverse is true of *good* actions. If someone we regard as one of "us" does a good deed, we will be inclined to explain what happened by attributing it to good character traits of the person in question. Daniel's giving a child a chocolate bar is described as an instance of "Daniel's generosity." Jerome's giving a child a chocolate bar is described in concrete terms: "That guy just gave that boy a chocolate bar."

Research on linguistic intergroup bias has shown that an audience can infer from how someone's actions are being described—abstractly or concretely—whether that person is being categorized as "us" or "them." For example, experimental subjects make inferences from the way someone describes someone else as to whether that person is likely to share the same political party as the person they are describing, or the same religion.[1] To describe someone as a "criminal" is both to mark that person with a terrifying permanent character trait and simultaneously to place the person outside the circle of "us." *They* are criminals. *We* make mistakes.

Politicians who describe whole categories of persons as "criminals" are imputing to them permanent character traits that are frightening to most people, while simultaneously positioning themselves as our protectors. Such language undermines the democratic process of reasonable decision making, replacing it with fear. Another salient example in the U.S. context is the use of the term "riot" to describe political protests. In the United States in the 1960s, the civil rights movement included black political protests in urban areas against police brutality (most famously in the Watts neighborhood of Los Angeles and the Harlem district of Manhattan). These protests were regularly described in the media as "riots." As James Baldwin wrote at the time about the media description of these protests, "when white men rise up against oppression, they are heroes: when black men rise, they have reverted to their native savagery. The uprising in the Warsaw ghetto was not described as a riot, nor were the participants maligned as hoodlums: the boys and girls in Watts and Harlem are thoroughly aware of this."[2] Such misrepresentations allowed Richard Nixon to run for office in 1968 on a "law and order" platform. Nixon's administration is generally viewed as laying the groundwork for the subsequent mass incarceration of black American citizens.

In 2015, widespread protests by largely black crowds against police brutality occurred in Baltimore after the killing of Freddie Gray by police. In an article for *Linguistic Pulse* in April 2015, Nic Subtirelu compared different media outlets' use of "protest" versus "riot" to describe the Baltimore protests. Subtirelu found that Fox News, the United States' far-right media outlet, used "riot" in its coverage of the Baltimore unrest with more than twice the frequency of its use of "protest." CNN, by contrast, used "riot" with only slightly more frequency than "protest," and MSNBC used "protest" with only slightly more frequency than "riot" in its coverage of the unrest in Baltimore.[3] The misrepresentation of political protests as riots was a factor in the election campaign of Donald

Trump, whose campaign had strong echoes of Nixon's. Nixon, however, campaigned at a time of rising rates of violent crime. Trump's successful "law and order" campaign took place under the conditions of some of the lowest rates of violent crime in recorded U.S. history.

. . .

Discussion that uses terms like "criminal" to encompass both those who commit multiple homicides for pleasure and those who commit traffic violations, or "riot" to describe a political protest, changes attitudes and shapes policy. A good example of what can result when language that criminalizes an entire group of people distorts debate and leads to unreasonable outcomes is the mass incarceration of American citizens of African descent.

In 1980, half a million Americans were in prison or jail. By 2013, there were more than 2.3 million. The explosion in incarceration has fallen disproportionately on American citizens who are the descendants of those who were enslaved in this country. White Americans constitute 77 percent of the U.S. population, and black Americans 13 percent. Yet more black Americans are incarcerated than white Americans. There has scarcely been a time in history when one group has composed so much of the world's prison population; black Americans may be only 13 percent of the U.S. population, but they are 9 percent of the *world's* prison population.

If the system of justice in the United States were fair, and if the 38 million black Americans were as prone to crime as the average ethnic group in the world (where an ethnic group is, for example, the 61 million Italians, or the 45 million Hindu Gujarati), you would expect that black Americans would also be about 9 percent of the 2013 estimated world population of 7.135 billion people. There would then be well over 600 million black Americans in the world. If you think that black Americans are like anybody else, then the nation of black America should be the third-largest nation on earth, twice as large as the United States. You can of course still think, in the face of these facts, that the United States' prison laws are fairly applied and color-blind. But if you do, you almost certainly must believe that black Americans are among the most dangerous groups in the multi-thousand-year history of human civilization.

In the United States, the steep increase in incarceration rates has accompanied a steep drop in crime. In a 2017 review essay, "The Impacts of Incarceration on Crime," its author, David Roodman, notes that the "59% per capita rise in incarceration between 1990 and 2010 accompanied a 42% drop in FBI-tracked 'index crimes.'"[4] And yet, as Roodman accurately notes, "researchers agree that putting more people behind bars added modestly, at most, to the fall in crime." For one thing, Canada has experienced a pattern very similar to the United States', with steeply dropping crime rates since the 1990s. However, Canada's incarceration rate did not rise alongside the United States' experiment in mass incarceration that continued through the 1990s. If there is an explanation for the general North American drop in crime since 1990 that explains the similar U.S. and Canadian decrease in crime, it is not increased incarceration.

The main reason that many researchers are dubious about a link between an increase in incarceration and a drop in crime rates is because studies indicate that incarceration itself contributes substantively to an increase in crime rates. Formerly incarcerated individuals have much greater difficulty finding employment; this effect is multiplied, as we shall see in the final chapter, for black Americans. Formerly incarcerated citizens also have a drastically lower civic participation rate; they effectively remove themselves from civil society.[5] Incarceration also has a negative impact on families of the incarcerated, increasing the likelihood of subsequent incarceration. Black Americans face greater risk of incarceration compared to whites for the same crime, as evidenced, for example, by the vastly different rates of incarceration for drug crimes. Studies also suggest that incarceration itself leads to crime—Roodman summarizes this effect as "more time in prison, more crime after prison."

But the more important question is why harshly punitive measures are considered an appropriate response to adverse social conditions among black Americans. When a community has a particularly high crime rate, there is clearly a social problem requiring empathy and understanding, and an urgent need for policies that address underlying structural causes. The more important question is then: What is the source of widespread lack of empathy for this group?

Pause for a moment in this context to consider the empathy in play when the contemporary "opiate crisis" is covered in the U.S. media. The opiate crisis is not depicted as driven by vicious and terrifying "opiate rings." Nor are those addicted to opiates defined as criminals. If anything, the media, politicians, social commentary, the medical community, and even President Trump address opiate addiction, yes, as a crisis, but as a public health epidemic and not as an issue directly tied to law and order. The opiate crisis is not associated with African American citizens; rather, it is associated with Trump's base, rural whites and displaced white industrial workers. In short, a complicated and compassionate public analysis of opiate addiction is in play in U.S. public discourse, and federal and state initiatives are focused on prevention and treatment. If only such an analysis had been applied to African American citizens when drug addiction appeared to be associated with them. The addiction of citizens of all races, classes, and groups should be addressed with compassion, empathy, and the liberal values of shared human dignity and equality.

In 1896, Frederick L. Hoffman published the book *Race Traits and Tendencies of the American Negro,* which the historian Khalil Gibran Muhammad describes as "arguably the most influential race and crime study of the first half of the twentieth century." Its thesis is that black Americans are uniquely violent, lazy, and prone to disease. In 1996, William J. Bennett, John J. DiIulio, Jr., and John P. Walters published the book *Body Count: Moral Poverty . . . and How to Win America's War Against Crime and Drugs*. Its thesis is that America faces a unique threat from a new generation of young men, a large percentage of whom are black, who are especially prone to cruel, violent acts and incapable of honest work; these young men they call "super-predators." The book warns of a coming wave of youth violence by these "super-predators" (the wave of course did not materialize; violent crime plummeted in subsequent years, rather than sharply rising). These two works bookend a century of pseudoscience forging a link in the American consciousness between criminality and Americans who descended from enslaved Africans. Despite the century-long gap between them, the two books are remarkably similar: Both employ the sober language of statistics to raise moral panic about a coming wave of racialized violence (*Body Count,* unlike Hoffman's book, grounds its false predictions in claims about the "moral poverty" of "inner-city culture," rather than genetics).

Essentially as long as there have been black Americans, they have been challenging the pseudoscientific attempt to "write crime into race." In his 1898 essay "The Study of the Negro Problems," W.E.B. Du Bois lamented the

> endless final judgments as to the American Negro emanating from men of influence and learning, in the very face of the fact known to every accurate student, that there exists today no sufficient material of proven reliability, upon which any scientist can base definite and final conclusions as to the present conditions and tendencies of the eight million American Negroes; and that any person or publication purporting to give such conclusions simply makes statements which go beyond the reasonably proven evidence.[6]

Du Bois here emphasizes the wide gap between what social scientists know and the full facts, a gap that is subject to what the Scottish philosopher Alasdair MacIntyre has called "manipulative expertise." Du Bois's words remain true today.

One particularly important example of manipulative expertise, both disturbing and revealing, is "super-predator theory," introduced, at least in its contemporary version, by a coauthor of *Body Count,* John DiIulio, Jr., a political science professor at Princeton at the time, in a successful attempt to advocate for adult prison sentences for juvenile offenders. The theory postulated a group of "super-predators" with intrinsically violent natures, who "kill, rape, maim, and steal without remorse" and for whom reform is not an option. In *Body Count* as well as other publications, DiIulio predicted a large increase in violent crime in the United States from 1995 to 2000 arising from the (mysterious) development of a rash of "super-predators" entering society. His prediction was treated as credible, despite the fact that violent crime in the United States began dropping in the early 1990s and continued to fall from 1995 to 2000. DiIulio spoke with much more certainty than the evidence warranted. One might suspect this to be a case in which a background ideology linking race and crime explains the large gap between the evidence at hand and how social scientists had interpreted it.

The theory had a large effect on public discourse. In the 1996 election, U.S. presidential candidates Bill Clinton and Bob Dole competed over who would be harsher on these "super-predators." Though its effects are hard to quantify, it seems clear the theory contributed greatly to the adoption of draconian and dubiously constitutional policies charging juveniles as adults. The asymmetrical racial application of these laws has been well documented; for example, a 2012 Sentencing Project report shows that 940 of the 1,579 survey respondents serving life without parole for crimes committed as juveniles were black. Super-predator theory has contributed to a public culture in which black juveniles are viewed as significantly more culpable than white juveniles.

Demagogic language does not just affect public discourse. It has well-documented, deep-seated effects on judgment and perception throughout a population. A criminal is someone whose character is deficient, who is by nature beyond society's help. Jennifer Eberhardt's work in social psychology has helped document the effects of 150 years of racial propaganda linking black Americans to irredeemable criminality. In a 2012 paper, Eberhardt, along with coauthors Aneeta Rattan, Cynthia Levine, and Carol Dweck, presented white subjects with factual information about a Supreme Court case deciding the constitutionality of life without parole for juvenile offenders.[7] In the materials the participants were given was a description of an example juvenile recipient, "a 14-year-old male with 17 prior juvenile convictions on his record who brutally raped an elderly woman." The juvenile was described either as "a black male" or "a white male." After being presented with this information, the participants were asked, "To what extent do you support life sentences with no possibility of parole for juveniles when they have been convicted of serious violent crimes (in which no one was killed)?" and were directed to rate their responses on a scale of 1 ("extremely") to 6 ("not at all"). Those who were given the description of the "14-year-old male" as black were significantly more likely to support life sentences with no possibility of parole for juveniles.

In a 2014 paper, "Racial Disparities in Incarceration Increase Acceptance of Punitive Policies," Eberhardt and coauthor Rebecca Hetey had a white female experimenter present white registered California voters with California's draconian three-strikes law, as well as a petition to amend it.[8] According to California's law, passed in 1994, if someone had two previous serious felonies, no matter how long ago they occurred, a "third strike" for a violation as small as stealing "a dollar in loose change from a parked car" would result in a mandatory sentence of twenty-five years to life imprisonment. The proposed petition would amend the law to require that the third strike be a violent crime.

Before presenting the subjects with the petition, the experimenter would show them a forty-second video with eighty mug shots of inmates, both black and white. In one video, 45 percent of the faces were black (the "more black condition"). In the other video, 25 percent of the faces were black (the "less black condition"). In the "less black condition," 51 percent of the subjects signed the petition. Only 27 percent signed the petition in the "more black condition." Eberhardt's work is only the latest in a large body of research showing that the mass incarceration of Americans of African descent has its roots in racist propaganda tracing back to the days of slavery that casts members of this group as irredeemably criminal. The result has been a massive overrepresentation, historic in scale, of this group in the U.S. prison population.

Fascist propaganda does not, of course, merely present members of targeted groups as criminals. To ensure the right kind of moral panic about these groups, its members are represented as particular *kinds* of threats to the fascist nation—most important, and most typical, a threat to its purity. Consequently, fascist politics also emphasizes one kind of crime. The basic threat that fascist propaganda uses to raise fear is that members of the targeted group will rape members of the chosen nation, thereby polluting its "blood." The threat of mass rape is simultaneously intended as a threat to the patriarchal norms of the fascist state, to the "manhood" of the nation. The crime of rape is basic to fascist politics because it raises *sexual anxiety,* and an attendant need for protection of the nation's manhood by the fascist authority.

8

SEXUAL ANXIETY

If the demagogue is the father of the nation, then any threat to patriarchal manhood and the traditional family undermines the fascist vision of strength. These threats include the crimes of rape and assault, as well as so-called sexual deviance. The politics of sexual anxiety is particularly effective when traditional male roles, such as that of family provider, are already under threat by economic forces.

Fascist propaganda promotes fear of interbreeding and race mixing, of corrupting the pure nation with, in the words of Charles Lindbergh, speaking for the America First movement, "inferior blood." Fascist propaganda characteristically magnifies this fear by sexualizing the threat of the other. Since fascist politics has, at its basis, the traditional patriarchal family, it is characteristically accompanied by panic about deviations from it. Transgender individuals and homosexuals are used to heighten anxiety and panic about the threat to traditional male gender roles.

. . .

In his 1970 article "The 'Black Horror on the Rhine': Race as a Factor in Post–World War I Diplomacy," the historian Keith Nelson documents the mass hysteria that gripped Germany about the African soldiers serving among the French troops that occupied the Rhineland starting in 1919.[1] German propaganda about the supposed mass rape of German women by French soldiers from African colonies was spread as widely as possible, and included pieces translated into nearly every European language, including Esperanto. The German government promulgated racial fantasies of mass rape of white women by black men as a means of fighting the French occupation. This propaganda was particularly successful in "the racially sensitive" United States. A group calling itself "the American Campaign Against the Horror on the Rhine" ran off ten thousand pamphlets using money "contributed by wealthy German- and Irish-Americans," and a rally against "The Horror on the Rhine" on February 28, 1921, attracted a crowd of twelve thousand to Madison Square Garden in New York City. Nelson writes:

> Likewise, a young German nationalist named Adolf Hitler could not forget the thought that "7,000,000

> [people] languish under alien rule and the main artery of German people flows through the playground of black African hordes. . . . It was and is the Jews who bring the Negro to the Rhine, always with the same concealed thought and the clear goal of destroying by the bastardization which would necessarily set in, the white race which they hate."

According to Hitler, Jews were behind a conspiracy to use black soldiers to rape pure Aryan women as a means of destroying the "white race." This was also a conspiracy theory shared by the American Ku Klux Klan in the 1920s, which fantasized openly about Jews intentionally plotting the mass rape of white women by black men to undermine the white race in the United States.

"In the history of the United States, the fraudulent rape charge stands out as one of the most formidable artifices invented by racism," writes the activist Angela Davis. "The myth of the Black rapist has been methodically conjured up whenever recurrent waves of violence and terror against the Black community have required convincing justification."[2] The practice of lynching black men in the United States was justified by alleging the necessity of defending the purity of white American women; in the words of the historian Crystal Feimster, "southern white men [actively mobilized] the image of the black rapist for their political advantage."[3] The South

Carolina senator Benjamin Tillman said on the floor of the Senate that "the poor African has become a fiend, a wild beast seeking whom he may devour, filling our penitentiaries and our jails, lurking around to see if some helpless white woman can be murdered or brutalized." It was not only white *men* whose sexual anxiety and demagoguery about black men led to the horrific multidecade spate of mass lynchings of black American men. Rebecca Latimer Felton was the first woman to be a U.S. senator, after a long career in the public eye, by appointment (for one day) in 1922. A distinguished proponent of (white) women's rights, she also poured fuel on the fire of racism in her career, going so far as to declare in an 1897 speech, about the putative danger of black rapists, "if it takes lynching to protect women's dearest possession from drunken, ravening beasts, then I say lynch a thousand times a week."

The great antilynching crusader Ida B. Wells attempted to counter this narrative in her two pamphlets, "Southern Horrors: Lynch Law in All Its Phases" (1892) and "A Red Record: Tabulated Statistics and Alleged Causes of Lynchings in the United States 1892-1893-1894" (1894). Wells's findings that the majority of lynching victims were not even so much as accused of rape were greeted with widespread incredulity, as many historians have documented.[4] Whites across the United States assumed that there was an epidemic of mass rape perpetrated by black men on white women that justified the horrors of lynching, because that would make rational sense of the fear and anxiety they felt over the potential loss of status associated with accepting their black fellow citizens as equals. Where sexual anxiety might seem extreme, paranoid, or abstract, there is often a more tangible insecurity lurking behind it.

These fears experienced in the United States in the nineteenth and twentieth centuries have been repeated around the world. In the fall of 2017, one of the worst campaigns of ethnic cleansing since the Second World War swept through Myanmar, targeting the Rohingya people of that country, a population of Muslims who do not share the majority Buddhist religion. Hundreds of Rohingya villages have been burned to the ground, and mass slaughter and brutal mass rape have led to the flight of over half a million Rohingyas to Bangladesh. The unspeakably barbaric campaign of ethnic cleansing against the Rohingya people has its recent origins in unrest that began in June 2012 with the rape and murder of a young Buddhist woman by several Rohingya men. In 2014, rumors on social media of the rape of another Buddhist woman led to more violence. In general, the genocide against the Rohingyas has been fueled by paranoid theories of Muslim sexual schemes to prey on Buddhist women; a 2014 article in the *Los Angeles Daily News* reporting on the situation is headlined BUDDHIST VIGILAN-

TES IN MYANMAR ARE SPARKING RIOTS WITH WILD RUMORS OF MUSLIM SEX PREDATORS. In interviews with experts on Myanmar, the article documents a decades-long history of Buddhist extremist propaganda about "Muslim men scheming for their women."

In India, Hindu nationalists have regularly stoked anti-Muslim sentiment with campaigns calling attention to the supposed threat Muslim men pose to Hindu masculinity. Most recently, this took the form of a panic about a supposed "love jihad." In an article in *Indian Express* in August 2014, the Indian historian Charu Gupta calls attention to "an aggressive, systematic campaign," including "awareness rallies," organized by RSS and some factions of the dominant Hindu nationalist party BJP, about the supposed "love jihad" movement, which according to the BJP, compelled Hindu women to convert to Islam by marriage and deception.[5] Gupta adds that these campaigns are based on divisive principles that are sustained by "constant and repetitive references to the aggressive and libidinal energies of the Muslim male, creating a common 'enemy other.'" She decries the loss of "Hindu logical faculties" in the face of a "politics of cultural virginity and a myth of innocence" that are "combined with a perceived 'illegitimacy' of the act, leading to rants of violation, invasion, seduction and rape."

In the United States at the moment of this writing, we

also see a loss of "logical faculties" in the face of a barrage of propaganda connecting immigrant groups to rape. Trump famously began his campaign by denouncing Mexican immigrants to the United States as rapists. In an article for *The New York Times* on September 26, 2017, Caitlin Dickerson wrote about what happened in the small town of Twin Falls, Idaho, where three refugee boys, aged seven, ten, and fourteen, were accused of some kind of sexual activity with a five-year-old American girl. Immediately after the incident, Facebook groups formed about it, with links to articles on the Internet claiming "that the little girl had been gang raped at knifepoint, that the perpetrators were Syrian refugees and that their fathers had celebrated with them afterward by giving them high fives." Soon thereafter, the headline article on the *Drudge Report,* one of the most visited sites on the Internet, screamed "REPORT: Syrian 'Refugees' Rape Little Girl at Knifepoint in Idaho." The articles were all false—for one thing, as Dickerson reports, no Syrian refugees were resettled in Twin Falls. It's not clear that there was any attack at all (a police officer, based on the cellphone video of the incident, called the Internet descriptions of it "100 percent false, like not even close to being accurate"). Nevertheless, the fake news stories created a wave of intimidating harassment against public officials in Twin Falls, and a storm of outrage against refugees in the community. In short, they created moral panic about the sexual danger refugees posed for American white girls, a panic that has yet to subside.

The rhetoric on immigration that surrounded the Trump campaign (and continues to surround his administration) parallels the tactics of Russian propaganda outlets, which have spread fake news stories (as well as grossly exaggerating facts) about Middle Eastern immigrants raping white women in Europe. To take just one example, discussed in a September 2017 *New York Times* article by Jim Rutenberg, Russian propaganda outlets tried to create a fake scandal about a supposed rape of a thirteen-year-old girl in Berlin by a Middle Eastern immigrant in 2016. Multiple media outlets produced stories about the supposed rape, stoking outrage among the German Russian community, ultimately to the point where seven hundred people gathered to protest an event that never occurred. Russian media coverage and Russian fake news stories inflamed outrage. The fact that all of this eerily mirrors the spread of the German propaganda campaign in the 1920s of "the Black Horror on the Rhine" should dissuade us from adopting the view, currently in vogue, that this sort of "fake news" is a consequence of the modern revolution in social media.

. . .

Patriarchal masculinity sets up men with the expectation that society will allow them the role of sole protectors and providers of their families. In times of extreme economic anxiety, men, already made anxious by a perceived loss of status resulting from increasing gender equality, can easily be thrust into panic by demagoguery directed against sexual minorities. Here fascist politics intentionally distorts the source of anxiety. (A fascist politician has no intention of addressing the root causes of economic hardship.) Fascist politics distorts male anxiety, heightened by economic anxiety, into fear that one's family is under existential threat from those who reject its structure and traditions. Here again, the weapon used in fascist politics is a supposed potential threat of sexual assault.

In March 2016, the General Assembly of North Carolina passed House Bill 2, the so-called Bathroom Bill. The bill mandates that local boards of education enforce "single-sex multiple occupancy bathrooms," meaning that transgender individuals had to use the bathroom of their birth sex (thus, a transgender girl would have to use a boy's bathroom). The entire debate surrounding the "bathroom bill" focused on the threat posed by transgender girls to cisgender (non-transgender) girls. Its sponsors and supporters pushed for the bill by arguing that transgender girls were likely sexual predators. The Republican governor of North Carolina, Pat McCrory, justified his decision to sign the bill by arguing that House Bill 2 was necessary to protect the women of North Carolina. Legislators in more than a dozen U.S. states in 2016 considered bathroom bills modeled after House Bill 2.

Julia Serano explains in her classic work *Whipping Girl* that trans women, because they *choose* femininity, pose a serious threat to patriarchal ideologies:

> In a male-centered gender hierarchy, where it is assumed that men are better than women and that masculinity is superior to femininity, there is no greater perceived threat than the existence of trans women, who despite being male and inheriting male privilege "choose" to be female instead. By embracing our own femaleness and femininity, we, in a sense, cast a shadow of doubt over the supposed supremacy of maleness and masculinity. In order to lessen the threat we pose to the male-centered gender hierarchy, our culture (primarily via the media) uses every tactic in its arsenal of traditional sexism to dismiss us.[6]

Since the original publication of Serano's book in 2007, rhetorical attacks on trans women have moved into the center of U.S. politics. Given the significance of gender hierarchy to fascist ideology, that politicians have been trying to foment mass hysteria about trans women is unsurprising if this effort is understood as a manifestation of fascist political tactics and a sign that fascist politics is ascendant. Conversely, the growing acceptance of trans women is a strong affirmation of liberal democratic norms.

Recall the importance of the patriarchal family to fascism: The fascist leader is analogous to the patriarchal father, the "CEO" of the traditional family. The role of the father in the patriarchal family is to protect the mother and the children. Attacking trans women, and representing the feared other as a threat to the manhood of the nation, are ways of placing the very idea of manhood at the center of political attention, gradually introducing fascist ideals of hierarchy and domination by physical power to the public sphere.

Mária Schmidt is a far-right Hungarian historian who is director of the Hungarian House of Terror museum in Budapest. In an article about Schmidt's 2017 book *Language and Freedom* that a linguistics professor at the University of Vienna, Johanna Laakso, published online in the Hungarian Spectrum, Laakso describes Schmidt's enemies as "Muslim immigrants, left-wing liberal elite, and George Soros."[7] In the same review, Laakso quotes from Schmidt's criticisms of Angela Merkel's decision to admit around one million Syrian refugees into Germany, and the country's reception of them. Schmidt writes:

> A normal man or boy will know his duties and defend his wife, daughter, mother, or sister. Only these Germans of today have turned so brain-washed and unmanly that they are not even capable of that.

Schmidt blames the acceptance of a large group of Syrian refugees into Germany on the decline of patriarchal gender roles in that country. What fills the large gap in logic in this explanation is Schmidt's assumption of a fascist mythic past before the decline, in which men played the supposedly traditional patriarchal gender role of "protecting" women from foreign influence.

Highlighting supposed threats to the ability of men to protect their women and children solves a difficult political problem for fascist politicians. In liberal democracy, a politician who explicitly attacks freedom and equality will not garner much support. The politics of sexual anxiety is a way to get around this issue, in the name of safety; it is a way to attack and undermine the ideals of liberal democracy without being seen as explicitly so doing.

By employing the politics of sexual anxiety, a political leader represents, albeit indirectly, freedom and equality as threats. The expression of gender identity or sexual preference is an exercise of freedom. By presenting homosexuals or transgender women as a threat to women and children—and, by extension, to men's ability to protect them—fascist politics impugns the liberal ideal of freedom. A woman's right to have an abortion is also an exercise of freedom. By representing abortion as a threat to children—and to men's control over them—fascist politics impugns the liberal ideal of freedom. A person's right to marry whom they wish is an exercise of freedom; by representing members of one religion, or one race, as a threat because of the possibility of intermarriage is to impugn the liberal ideal of freedom.

The politics of sexual anxiety also undermines equality. When equality is granted to women, the role of men as sole providers for their families is threatened. Highlighting male helplessness in the face of sexual threats to their wives and children accentuates such feelings of anxiety at the loss of patriarchal masculinity. The politics of sexual anxiety is a powerful way to present freedom and equality as fundamental threats without explicitly appearing to reject them. A robust presence of a politics of sexual anxiety is perhaps the most vivid sign of the erosion of liberal democracy.

Politicians, then, turn their attention to the sites of the most egregious and concentrated sources of sexual deviance and violent threats—cosmopolitan urban centers. In the book of Genesis, Sodom and Gomorrah are cities that are singled out by God to be destroyed for their wickedness and sin. There is textual controversy over what sins were said to be the reason for the destruction of these cities. But regardless of scholarship, in the historical imagination, the sins have been taken to be sexual in nature, specifically, homosexuality. Cities have long been treated, in rhetoric and literature, as places of decadence and sin, most particularly, sexual decadence and sin. Sodom and Gomorrah are the biblical reference points for the source of sexual anxiety, where homosexuality, race mixing, and other sins against fascist ideology are most likely to occur.

9

SODOM AND GOMORRAH

That afternoon, at the former officer's dacha, I learned to shoot from the man who raises rabbits for food but does not have the heart to kill them. The animal lover, discussing the cultural attitudes that make this region distinctive, explained it thus: "for example, if homosexuals arrived in our town, we would kill them."

—Nicholas Muellner, *In Most Tides an Island*

Chapter 1 of *Mein Kampf* is titled "My Home." It is a short chapter, a mere three and a half pages. In it, Hitler pays homage to his birthplace, Braunau on the Inn, a "little town [that] lies on the frontier between the two German states," suffused with German nationalist pride and industrious, hardworking people. Sadly, "poverty and stern reality" led him away from his idyllic small town home, and "with a valise full of clothes and linen I went to Vienna full of determination."

The second chapter of *Mein Kampf,* "My Studies and Struggles in Vienna," concerns Hitler's experience with Austria's largest and most cosmopolitan city. Vienna, according to its first page, is a "poisonous snake"; to "get to know its poison fangs," one must live there. Hitler describes Vienna as a city dominated and controlled by Jews, who lambaste and insult traditional German culture in favor of a sickeningly decadent facsimile. Hitler decries the lack of German national pride in Vienna. Most of all, Hitler despises Vienna for its cosmopolitanism, its mixture of different cultural and racial groups: "I hated the mixture of races displayed in the capital. I hated the motley collection of Czechs, Poles, Hungarians, Ruthenians, Serbs, Croats, and above all that ever-present fungoid growth—Jews and again Jews."[1] In Germany, there was a romantic tradition in literature and culture that took cities to be the cause of social ills, and the countryside as a purifying element. National Socialist ideology took this to extremes: Pure German values were rural values, realized in peasant life; the cities, by contrast, were sites of racial defilement, where pure Nordic blood was ruined by mixture with others. As Hitler writes in the second chapter of his unpublished Second Book:

> . . . a particular danger of the so-called peaceful economic policy of a people lies in the fact that it initially

> enables an increase in the population that will no longer be in proportion to the productivity of the people's own land and territory. Not infrequently, this crowding of too many people into an inadequate Lebensraum also leads to difficult social problems. People are now gathered into work centers that do not resemble cultural sites as much as abscesses on the body of the people—places where all evils, vices, and sicknesses appear to unite. They are above all hotbeds of blood-mixing and bastardization, usually ensuring the degeneration of the race and resulting in that purulent herd in which the maggots of the international Jewish community flourish and cause the ultimate decay of the people.[2]

Hitler's denunciations of large cosmopolitan cities, and their cultural productions, is standard in fascist politics. "Hollywood," or its local proxy, often supposedly controlled by Jews, is always destroying traditional values and culture by producing "perverted" art. In the 1930 manifesto of the Kampfbund für deutsche Kultur (the official National Socialist "fighting society" for German culture), Alfred Rosenberg issues a "call for resistance to all tendencies in the theater which are damaging to the people, for the theater in nearly all big cities today has become the scene of perverted instincts. We fight against a constantly spreading corruption of our concepts of justice, a corruption which gives the big swindlers practically a free hand in exploiting the people."[3]

. . .

Whereas cities, to the fascist imagination, are the source of corrupting culture, often produced by Jews and immigrants, the countryside is pure. The "Official Party Statement on Its Attitude toward the Farmers and Agriculture" was published in the National Socialist *Völkischer Beobachter* in 1930, with Hitler's signature (though its actual authorship is unclear). It contains a concise statement of the Nazi ideology that the true values of the nation were to be found in the rural population, that National Socialists "see in the farmers the main bearers of a healthy folkish heredity, the fountain of youth of the people, and the backbone of military power." In fascist politics, the family-farm is the cornerstone of the nation's values, and family farm communities provide the backbone of its military.[4] Resources that flow to cities must be directed to the rural communities instead, to preserve this vital center of the nation's values. And the rural communities, as the source of the pure blood of the nation, cannot be polluted by outside blood via immigration. It was official Nazi policy that "by bettering the lot of the domestic agricultural laborer and by preventing flight from the land, the importation of foreign agricultural labor becomes unnecessary and will therefore be forbidden."[5]

A June 2017 *Washington Post*–Kaiser Foundation survey of almost seventeen hundred Americans found that "attitudes toward immigrants form one of the widest gulfs between U.S. cities and rural communities."[6] Forty-two percent of rural residents in the poll agreed with the statement "Immigrants are a burden on our country because they take our jobs, housing and health care." Only 16 percent of urban residents agreed with this characterization of immigrants as burdensome. The poll suggests that the politics of rural versus urban is a promising avenue for sowing division for demagogically minded U.S. politicians, particularly around the topic of immigration.

An article for *The Guardian* published on April 21 during the 2017 presidential election in France describes the base for Le Front National, and its presidential candidate, Marine Le Pen, as "people living in modest towns and country villages far away from big cities." Le Pen's message of "hardline security and anti-immigration" are characterized as responsible for a surge in rural support for her party, where anti-immigration sentiment is deep and pervasive "even where immigration is very scarce." In the first round of voting, despite receiving less than 5 percent of the vote in Paris, France's capital and largest city, Le Pen finished a close second to Emmanuel Macron, with "regional results pointed to political fracturing between the big cities and more rural areas."[7] In the final round, which Emmanuel Macron won in a landslide, the rural/urban split remained. An article on May 12, 2017, in the BBC summarized their differences in support:

> Mr Macron scored best in the big cities, including Paris where nine out of 10 voters backed him. It was his strongest area of support. In contrast, Ms Le Pen's biggest support came from the countryside.[8]

Similarly, during the 2016 presidential election in the United States, Donald Trump's harsh anti-immigration rhetoric was particularly popular in rural areas with very few immigrants.

. . .

Fascist politics aims its message at the populace outside large cities, to whom it is most flattering. It is especially resonant during times of globalization, when economic power swings to the large urban areas as centers of an emerging global economy, as occurred in the 1930s in Europe. Fascist politics highlights the wrongs a globalized economy does to rural areas, adding to it a focus on traditional rural values of self-sufficiency supposedly put at risk by the success of liberal cities culturally and economically.

In the 2014 elections for the state legislature in Minnesota, a Republican wave upended the Democratic majority. In a January 25, 2015, *Star Tribune* article explaining the Republican triumph, in which one Democrat was derided as "Metro Jay" by his Republican opponent, Patrick Condon writes on numerous local and national issues, including a new state senate office building in St. Paul, the legalization of gay marriage, and efforts to bring the Affordable Care Act to Minnesota, Republican candidates in many of the state's furthest reaches capitalized on unease that big-city Democrats were inflicting their values on small towns while hoarding the spoils of the state treasury.

The pervasive sense that city dwellers in Minnesota were living off the taxes of the hardworking rural population of Minnesota was a powerful force in the Minnesota Republican triumph in 2014. ("We pay taxes too," Cordon quotes a rural Minnesota resident as saying, "but we see a lot of our tax dollars going to urban development in the metro area. We'd like to see some of that share. We'd like to have nice roads too.") And yet, as is typical in politics that exacerbates the rural-urban divide during times of globalization, the perception was mythical—in Minnesota, as in many places in the globalized economy, it is the metro areas that are "the state's economic engine, generating tax dollars that flow outward to every corner of the state."

Fascist politics feeds the insulting myth that hardworking rural residents pay to support lazy urban dwellers, so it is not a surprise that the base of its success is found in a country's rural areas. In a 1980 essay on the composition of support for the Nazi Party, "The Electoral Geography of the Nazi Landslide," Nico Passchier notes that "rural, and especially agrarian, support for Nazism was extensive" and that the Nazis had "special success in areas with small farms, a rather homogeneous social structure, strong feelings of local solidarity, and social control."[9]

The accuracy of a fascist politician's attacks on cities is not particularly important to their success. These messages resonate with voters who do not live in cities, and they don't need to appeal to urban dwellers. Anticity rhetoric had a central role in the 2016 U.S. presidential elections. Violent crime rates in the United States in 2016 and 2017 were near historic lows (the most salient instances of violent crimes—mass shootings—were not specifically connected to urban areas and were usually committed by white men). Cities were thriving; the "millennial generation" in the United States tended to prefer urban to suburban areas, and urban areas were experiencing a tremendous revival. Many areas that in the 1970s and 1980s were the paradigm of blighted urban ghettos, such as Harlem, had experienced, for good or for ill, tremendous gentrification and steeply escalating housing prices. Despite this, U.S. president Donald Trump, during the 2016 U.S. presidential campaign and afterward, regularly spoke of American cities as sites of carnage and blight. For example, in a tweet on January 14, 2017, then president-elect Trump spoke of "burning and crime-infested inner cities of the U.S." Despite remarkable gentrification in American cities, Trump regularly speaks of cities as containing ghettos filled with black people (who, he implies, are likely criminals). A typical line from one of his campaign speeches was "Our African-American communities are absolutely in the worst shape that they've ever been in before, ever, ever, ever. You take a look at the inner cities, you get no education, you get no jobs, you get shot walking down the street." And yet during this time, cities in the United States were enjoying their lowest rates of crime in generations and record low unemployment. Trump's rhetoric about cities makes sense in the context of a more general fascist politics, in which cities are seen as centers of disease and pestilence, containing squalid ghettos filled with despised minority groups living off the work of others.

. . .

The appeal to the countryside in fascist politics can be obscured in countries with urban centers containing deeply religious neighborhoods, or neighborhoods with impoverished workers from rural areas who are well served by the populist economic policies favored by some authoritarian leaders. Recep Tayyip Erdoğan began his national political career as the mayor of Istanbul, Turkey's largest city. Istanbul has large neighborhoods dominated by conservative religious voters, which provided him with an early base of support; Erdoğan's populist economic policies also served Istanbul's neglected poor well. However, in 1999, Erdoğan chose Siirt, "a town in the religiously conservative and restive southeastern part of the country," to give a controversial antisecular speech that landed him in prison for "inciting hatred based on religious difference."[10] As Erdoğan increasingly engaged in fascist politics, his base of support has swung to rural areas. All three of Turkey's largest cities voted against the 2017 referendum granting Erdoğan virtually dictatorial powers. The referendum passed only because of his strong support outside these centers.

Large urban centers tend toward particularly high degrees of pluralism. In cities, one is likely to find not just the greatest degree of ethnic and religious diversity, but also the greatest diversity of lifestyles and customs. The literature on National Socialism supports the view that urban areas brought with them a measure of tolerance that served to protect, at least for a while, the populations targeted by the Nazis. According to Richard Grunberger,

"Jews living in villages and small towns were subjected to window smashing and physical assault, sometimes culminating in murder. This made them seek the anonymity and sense of communal comfort to be found in large centres like Frankfurt and Berlin. . . . Country areas generally tended to be more anti-Semitic than urban ones. In the cities, anti-Jewish feeling was roughly inversely proportional to [the city's] size."[11]

Fascist ideology rejects pluralism and tolerance. In fascist politics, everyone in the chosen nation shares a religion and a way of life, a set of customs. The diversity, with its concomitant tolerance of difference, in large urban centers is therefore a threat to fascist ideology. Fascist politics targets financial elites, "cosmopolitans," liberals, and religious, ethnic, and sexual minorities. In many countries, these are characteristically urban populations. Cities therefore usefully serve as a proxy target for the classic enemies of fascist politics.

. . .

In fascist ideology, the rural life is guided by an ethos of self-sufficiency, which breeds strength. In rural communities, one does not need to depend on the state, unlike the "parasites" in the city. Hitler writes that a lesson he learned from his time in Vienna was that "the social task may never consist of welfare work, which is both ridiculous and useless, but rather in removing the deep-seated mistakes in the organization of our economic and cultural life which are bound to end in degradation of the individual."[12] Richard Walther Darré was a leading Nazi ideologue and one of the most senior commanders of the SS. The thesis of Darré's 1929 essay "The Peasantry as the Key to Understanding the Nordic Race" is that true freedom is realized only in the rural agrarian life of the peasant. In the rural life, one is forced to "rely on one's own abilities" and be self-sufficient, rather than to be a "parasite," as Darré argues city-dwellers are.[13]

In fascism, the *state* is an enemy; it is to be replaced by the nation, which consists of self-sufficient individuals who collectively choose to sacrifice for a common goal of ethnic or religious glorification. In a tension that we will explore in the next chapter, fascist ideology involves something at least superficially akin to the libertarian ideal of self-sufficiency and freedom from "the state."

To boost the nation, fascist movements are obsessed with reversing declining birthrates; large families raised by dedicated homemakers are the goal.[14] In fascist politics, cities are denounced as sites of declining birthrates, which are blamed on the supposed weakening effect of cosmopolitanism on a population, making men and women less capable of fulfilling traditional gender roles (as soldiers and mothers, for example). In a 1927 speech by the Italian fascist leader Benito Mussolini, he writes,

> "At a certain point the city starts growing in a diseased, pathological way, not through its own resources but through external support. . . . The increasing infertility of citizens stands in a direct relationship to the rapid and monstrous growth of the cities. . . . The metropolis spreads, attracting the population from the countryside which, immediately it has become urbanized, becomes sterile just like the population which is already there. . . . The city dies, the nation . . . is now made up of people who are old and degenerate and cannot defend itself against a younger people which launches an attack on the now unguarded frontiers."[15]

Mussolini denounces the world's great cities, such as New York, for their teeming populations of nonwhites. In fascist ideology, the city is a place where members of the nation go to age and die, childless, surrounded by the vast hordes of despised others, breeding out of control, their children permanent burdens on the state.

Cities, in the fascist worldview, are collective enterprises where people rely on public infrastructure, "the state," for survival and comfort. Residents of cities do not hunt or grow their food, as in fascist mythology; they purchase it at stores. This runs counter to the fascist ideal of rural agrarian self-sufficiency. In fascist ideology, it is the nation that provides, not the state—small ethnically or religiously pure communities composed of self-sufficient individuals working as a community. We find clear evidence of this ideology in the contemporary United States as well. In the 2017 poll discussed on page 145, there was also a particularly large gulf between rural and urban respondents to the poll surrounding notions of hard work and self-sufficiency. When asked "In your opinion, which is generally more often to blame if a person is poor?" Forty-nine percent of rural residents agreed with the response "lack of effort on their own part," while 46 percent agreed with the response "difficult circumstances beyond their control." In contrast, only 37 percent of urban residents agreed with the response "lack of effort on their own part," whereas 56 percent agreed with "difficult circumstances beyond their control."

Fascist politics characteristically represents the minority populations living in cities as rodents or "parasites" living off the honest hard work of rural populations. As Hitler writes in *Mein Kampf*:

> Originally the Aryan was probably a nomad and then, as time went on, he became settled; this, if nothing else, proves that he was never a Jew! No, the Jew is not a nomad, for even the nomad had already a definite attitude towards the conception "work." . . . In the Jew, however, that conception has no place; he was never a

> nomad, but was ever a parasite in the bodies of other nations.[16]

In the National Socialist education system, "Jews are not seen in the occupations of factory worker, bricklayer, blacksmith, locksmith, miner, farmer, plasterer. In other words, the Jew avoided work with his hands and avoided heavy labor while 'living off the sweat of his neighbors. He is a parasite, like the mistletoe on a tree.'"[17] In fascist politics, the laziness of minorities in cities is cured only by forcing them into hard labor. Hard labor, in Nazi ideology, had a remarkable power: It could purify an inherently lazy race.

10

ARBEIT MACHT FREI

In 2017, successive hurricanes of enormous strength hit the United States. In August, Hurricane Harvey devastated the city of Houston, in the state of Texas. In September, Hurricane Maria had a considerably worse impact on the U.S. territory of Puerto Rico, many of whose residents were left for months without power. Those born in Puerto Rico, like those born in Houston, are American citizens. And yet the difference between the reaction to the hurricanes was extreme, both federally, from President Trump, and among many white Americans living on the mainland United States. In an October 2017 article in *The Washington Post* by Jenna Johnson headlined MANY TRUMP VOTERS WHO GOT HURRICANE RELIEF IN TEXAS AREN'T SURE PUERTO RICANS SHOULD, she quotes Fred Maddox, a seventy-five-year-old Houston resident, on the topic of whether Puerto Rico should receive the kind of federal aid that Houston did:

> It shouldn't be up to us, really. I don't think so. He's trying to wake them up: Do your job. Be responsible.

The Maddox family did not have flood insurance but nevertheless received $14,000 in federal aid from FEMA. The article ends with a quote about Maddox's view of President Trump's differential responses to the disaster:

> He likes having a businessman in office, especially one who's not afraid to speak the painful truth.
>
> "It's time," he said, "we had someone in there to fight for us."

In fascist ideology, in times of crisis and need, the state reserves support for members of the chosen nation, for "us" and not "them." The justification is invariably because "they" are lazy, lack a work ethic, and cannot be trusted with state funds and because "they" are criminal and seek only to live off state largesse. In fascist politics, "they" can be cured of laziness and thievery by hard labor. This is why the gates of Auschwitz had emblazoned on them the slogan ARBEIT MACHT FREI—work shall make you free.

In Nazi ideology, Jews were lazy, corrupt criminals who spent their time scheming to take the money of hardworking Aryans, a job that was facilitated by the state. The 1919 "Guidelines" of the Deutsche Arbeiterpartei (DAP)–the German Workers' Party, the original name of the Nazi Party—ask "Who is the DAP fighting against?" The answer is "Against all those who create no value, who make high profits without any mental or physical work. We fight against the drones in the state; these are mostly Jews; they live a good life, they reap where they have not sown."[1] Their remedy was to dismantle the state and replace it with the nation. In contrast to the state, the nation lacks mechanisms like "welfare," which Hitler denounces for robbing individuals of their capacity for economic independence. The state represented the redistribution of the wealth of hardworking citizens to "undeserving" minorities outside the dominant ethnic or religious community, who would take advantage of them.

There is a large amount of social scientific work on white American support for "welfare" programs (a somewhat ill-defined category, in point of fact). Most often American opposition to welfare is represented as a manifestation of a commitment to individualism, of support and desire for nurturing an ethic of self-sufficiency. And yet a dominant theme emerging from research on white Americans' attitude toward welfare is that the single largest predictor of white Americans' attitude toward programs described as "welfare" is their attitude toward the judgment that black people are lazy. As the Princeton political scientist Martin Gilens writes in his 1996 paper "'Race Coding' and White Opposition to Welfare," "The perception that blacks are lazy has a larger effect on white Americans' welfare policy preferences than does economic self-interest, beliefs about individualism or views about the poor in general."[2]

Of course, variables such as racism, the belief that the poor are lazy, and endorsement of certain forms of individualism are not independent of one another. Many white Americans hold false beliefs about who is poor. There is widespread ignorance of the fact that the majority of those who benefit from welfare programs are white. Furthermore, as in the previous chapter, the valorization of self-sufficiency is at the core of fascist ideology, inextricably intermingled with hostility toward certain hated minority groups. We might distinguish between respective beliefs in the laziness of black people and of poor people and in the value of self-sufficiency. But in those susceptible to fascist ideology, they often come together.

In fascist ideology, the ideal of hard work is weaponized against minority populations. The French neofascist party Le Front National is viciously anti-immigrant. Party representatives regularly lambaste immigrants as lazy freeloaders living off the hard work and diligence of the "true" French people. For example, Marine Le Pen, its current head, said on the 2017 presidential campaign trail that "interlopers from all over the world . . . want to transform France into a giant squat."

• • •

The "hard work" versus "laziness" dichotomy is, like "law-abiding" versus "criminal," at the heart of the fascist division between "us" and "them." But what is most terrifying about these rhetorical divides is that it is typical of fascist movements to attempt to transform myths about "them" into reality through social policy. We see this regularly with movements of refugees. Hannah Arendt writes:

> It was always a too little noted hallmark of fascist propaganda that it was not satisfied with lying but deliberately proposed to transform its lies into reality. Thus, Das Schwarze Korps conceded several years before the outbreak of the war that people abroad did not completely believe the Nazi contention that all Jews are homeless beggars who can only subsist as parasites in the economic organism of other nations; but foreign public opinion, they prophesied, would in a few years be given the opportunity to convince itself of this fact when the German Jews would be driven out across the borders like a pack of beggars. For such a fabrication of

> a lying reality no one was prepared. The essential characteristic of fascist propaganda was never its lies, for this is something more or less common to propaganda everywhere and of every time. The essential thing was that they exploited the age-old Occidental prejudice which confuses reality with truth, and made that "true" which until then could only be stated as a lie.[3]

Traumatized, penniless refugees coming en masse across borders require state aid and support before entering labor markets. They require such support to learn the language and, initially at least, for shelter, food, and job training. By subjecting members of a despised minority to brutal treatment and then sending them as refugees across borders into other countries, fascist movements can create an apparent reality underlying their claim that members of that group are lazy and dependent on state aid or petty crime. By such methods, they also export the conditions that make fascist politics effective.

Arendt's point is that fascist unreality is a promissory note on the way to a future reality that transforms into fact at least some basis of what was once stereotyped myth. Fascist unreality is, as Arendt explains, a prelude to fascist policy. Fascist politics and fascist policy cannot easily be divorced from each other. The strong temptation for those who employ fascist politics, once they assume power, is to use their position of power to make their once fantastical statements increasingly more plausible.

In this way, as a prelude to ethnic cleansing or genocide, governments will artificially create the conditions inside the state that seem to legitimize the subsequent brutal treatment of the population. A good example is the Slovak state, led by Jozef Tiso, that emerged after Nazi Germany invaded Czechoslovakia in 1939. In his 2015 book, *Black Earth: The Holocaust as History and Warning*, the Yale historian Timothy Snyder writes:

> During the transition from Czechoslovak to Slovak law, Slovaks and others stole with enthusiasm from the Jews. Tiso and the leaders of the new state saw this as part of a natural process whereby Slovaks would displace Jews (and, in some measure, Slovak Catholics would displace Slovak Protestants) as the middle class. Laws expropriating Jews thus created an artificial Jewish question: what to do with all of these impoverished people?[4]

Snyder subsequently explains that the solution Slovak leaders chose was to deport their Jewish population to Auschwitz, after first seeking assurances from the Nazi leader Heinrich Himmler that the fifty-eight thousand Slovakian Jews they sent would not be returned.

The 2017 Rohingya crisis of ethnic cleansing and mass murder did not occur out of the blue. As written earlier, it began in earnest in 2012, after the rape and murder of a Buddhist woman by several Rohingya men, after which many Rohingyas were sequestered in hundreds of villages and prohibited from traveling. According to the June 2016 report of the United Nations high commissioner for human rights, starting in 2012, the majority of Rohingyas

> require official authorization to move between, and often within, townships (in northern Rakhine State, for example, a village departure certificate is required to stay overnight in another village). The procedures to secure travel are onerous and time-consuming. Failure to comply with requirements can result in arrest and prosecution. Restrictions routinely lead to extortion and harassment by law enforcement and public officials. . . . Protracted displacement, overcrowding in camps, the lack of livelihoods and constraints on all aspects of life exacerbate tensions and the risk of domestic violence.[5]

The treatment of the Rohingya minority in Myanmar robbed them of opportunities to work, and the constant harassment and policing no doubt created a mental health crisis among the population. All of this served to reinforce negative stereotypes of Rohingya people, which served to legitimize the brutal and inhumane treatment of them that culminated in the 2017 ethnic cleansing of their population as well as raising opposition to their acceptance as refugees in other lands.

Frantz Fanon, a psychiatrist by training, was born in Martinique and lived in both France and North Africa. Fanon's 1952 *Black Skin, White Masks,* published when he was only twenty-seven, is one of the classic anticolonial texts of the twentieth century. In a description of how French police treat Algerians, Fanon concisely spells out how the regular practice of the colonizer—in this case, the French police in Algeria—can create the material conditions underlying a racist stereotype.

The French stereotype of Arabs was that they were shifty, sneaky, dirty, and distrustful. But Fanon points out that this stereotype was created by the way that the French police regularly treated Arabs, and the fact that French rule impoverished them. Anyone would have a "hunted, evasive look of distrust" when they were subject to regularly being stopped by police in broad daylight. This is the only natural response to such treatment. The practice of French police itself caused colonial subjects to behave in a way that accorded with the stereotype. Summarizing the situation, Fanon concludes, "It is the racist who creates the inferiorized."[6]

. . .

The United States has its own history of policies that feed stereotypes and make them appear real. The structure of policing and incarceration, and the white reaction to them, is central to explaining how racialized mass incarceration in the United States constructs and seemingly legitimates negative group stereotypes. The chance of being incarcerated at least once in one's lifetime is one in three for black American men; it is one in seventeen for white American men. But the tragedy of this statistic does not end with an incarcerated person's release from prison. Those who have experienced incarceration face dauntingly difficult job prospects. A history of incarceration functions like a scarlet letter for employers. In a 2003 study demonstrating the devastating effects of prior incarceration on the search for employment, the Harvard University sociologist Devah Pager writes that incarceration becomes a label for individuals, much as college graduates or welfare recipients.

> The "negative credential" associated with a criminal record represents a unique mechanism of stratification, in that it is the state that certifies particular individuals in ways that qualify them for discrimination or social exclusion.[7]

In her landmark study, Pager discovered large effects of prior incarceration on employment opportunity. She used teams of auditors, two of whom were black and two of whom were white, with similar appearances and résumés. One member was told to report an eighteen-month incarceration for cocaine trafficking, and the other was told to report no criminal record. Each week, the team member who reported a criminal record would switch. Together, the teams applied for entry-level jobs in Milwaukee, Wisconsin.

Among whites, a criminal record reduced the likelihood of a callback interview for an entry-level job by 50 percent—Pager's white auditors who reported no criminal record had a 34 percent callback rate, and her white auditors who reported a criminal record had a 17 percent callback rate. The black auditors she used, with very similar résumés, had a 14 percent callback rate when they did not report a criminal record—suggesting that black Americans who report no criminal record already fare worse in seeking entry-level employment than white Americans who do report a criminal record. Only 5 percent of black applicants reporting a criminal record received callback interviews. According to Pager's study, both race and previous incarceration record have a drastic effect on one's employment chances. Adding race and previous incarceration record together makes employment prospects dramatically worse. Rising incarceration rates among black populations can naturally be expected to lead to rising unemployment among that population.

White American stereotypes of black Americans as lazy and violent derive from the very beginning of the

United States, where these attributes were regularly used to justify the enslavement of America's black population. After slavery, these stereotypes were used to justify the equally brutal practice of convict leasing, whereby large portions of the black population of the formerly antebellum South were arrested for petty crimes and leased to iron, steel, and coal companies for hard labor, often with fatal consequences.[8] The mechanisms underlying the racialized mass incarceration of black Americans are part of a long tradition of justifying stereotypes of this population as lazy—that is, unable, because supposedly unwilling, to gain employment.

In the 1960s, the Kennedy and Johnson administrations responded to the civil rights movement by pairing job training and antipoverty programs with punitive anticrime measures. When Richard Nixon ran for the office of president in 1968, he used urban unrest to change the subject from social justice to law and order. He did so at a time of salient moments of urban unrest but declining incarceration rates. Historian Elizabeth Hinton writes:

> When Richard Nixon took office in 1969, he inherited a penal system that had been shedding prisoners. The 1960s produced the single largest reduction in the population of federal and state prisons in the nation's history, with 16,500 fewer inmates in 1969 than in 1950. Despite this trend toward decarceration, under the aus-

pices of the Nixon administration the federal government began to construct prisons at unprecedented rates.[9]

In turning the nation's attention to law and order, the Nixon administration successfully made the case to drop Johnson's antipoverty programs and job initiatives, focusing instead on punitive crime measures, especially in urban centers populated by African Americans. Hinton and others provide strong reasons to believe that Nixon and members of his administration were well aware that their policies were going to lead to dramatically increased incarceration among black citizens. There are disagreements and open questions in the now large body of literature on the causes of the current crisis in mass incarceration in the United States. But there is no disagreement that the combination of harsh, punitive crime policies for black American communities coupled with drastic cuts to social welfare programs and job training has led to tragic consequences and a self-reinforcing pattern of repeated stereotypes and policies. In addition to the clear link between incarceration and the inability to get jobs, the combination of severe cuts to the social safety net and job programs and punitive crime polices has led to a population of black Americans with stubbornly high unemployment rates. Pointing to this population, politicians employing fascist tactics can speak of a crisis of laziness supposedly underlying multigenerational poverty, rather than to its real causes. The "laziness" can then supposedly be "cured" by forcing this population into "hard work" by slashing the safety net further. Given that the evidence suggests whites are not hiring black men, especially formerly incarcerated ones, this would then simply further entrench such patterns of unemployment—thereby perpetuating a flawed stereotype that is useful in fascist politics.

In the 1970s, the effects of this combination of policies were unclear. It was possible to think that harshly punitive anticrime measures were better than nothing to deal with persistent social problems such as violence and unemployment. We now know that aggressive anticrime measures targeted at minority populations paired with reduced social services to support their communities will lead to disastrous consequences. There have been years of media attention to the disaster of the policies emerging from the "tough on crime" movements of the 1970s, 1980s, and 1990s, resulting in large bipartisan support for shifting from punitive crime policies to social programs. However, what has not accompanied this shift is an awareness that the underlying motivations for the hard-on-crime rhetoric and policies were fascist, set up to establish an us-versus-them dichotomy and reinforce preexisting hierarchal stereotypes.

It should therefore concern U.S. citizens that at the

time of this writing, the plan of many members of the ruling Republican Party in the United States, including the administration of current U.S. president Donald Trump, his attorney general, Jeff Sessions, and Speaker of the House Paul Ryan, is to eliminate the already threadbare U.S. social welfare state while simultaneously making the criminal justice system substantially more punitive. After years and years of media attention to the consequences of such policies, no one can now claim ignorance of the effects of such a combination of policies, both on black Americans and on white racial attitudes. It takes studious ignorance of the facts, what the University of Connecticut philosopher Lewis Gordon calls "bad faith," to recommit to such failed policies.[10] Such "bad faith" is, as we have seen, characteristic of fascist regimes. We can see, in the case of U.S. politicians' attitudes toward crime policy and social welfare programs, that this willful ignorance is not benign. It has an unstated purpose—to create the conditions that allow racist stereotypes to flourish, so that politicians can continue to exploit fascist tactics for electoral gain.

. . .

One roadblock to the kind of us/them divisions described above is unity and empathy along class lines, exemplified in labor unions. In functioning unions, white working-class citizens identify with black working-class citizens rather than resent them. Fascist politicians understand the effectiveness of this solidarity to resisting divisive policies and therefore seek to dismantle unions. Despite its condemnation of "elites," fascist politics seeks to minimize the importance of class struggle.

The labor union is the chief mechanism societies have found to bind people who differ along various dimensions. Trade unions are sources of cooperation and community, and of wage equality, as well as mechanisms to provide protections from the vicissitudes of the global market. According to fascist politics, unions must be smashed so that individual laborers are left to fend for themselves on the sea of global capitalism, ready to become dependent instead on a party or leader. Antipathy to labor unions is such a major theme of fascist politics that fascism cannot be fully comprehended without an understanding of it.

In part 1 of *Mein Kampf,* Hitler repeatedly attacks trade unions. For example, he writes, "[The Jew] is gradually assuming leadership of the trades-union movement—all the easier because what matters to him is not so much genuine removal of social evils as the formation of a blindly obedient fighting force in industry for the purpose of destroying national economic independence" (131). In the chapter in *Mein Kampf* entitled "The Trades-Union Question" (evocative of "The Jewish Question"), Hitler writes that "Marxism forged [the trades-union system] into an instrument for its own class war. Marxism created the economic weapon which the international Jew employs for destroying the economic basis of free and independent national States, for ruining their national industry and trade." Hitler denounces trade unions, claiming they "hinder efficiency in business and in the life of the whole nation."[11] He calls for trade unions to be repurposed to serve the nation rather than class interests.

Concern for economic independence and business efficiency was only a mask for Hitler's real antipathy toward labor unions. Chapter 10 of Hannah Arendt's 1951 classic work *The Origins of Totalitarianism* is titled "A Classless Society." In that chapter, Arendt argues that fascism requires the individuals in a society to be "atomized," that is, to lose their mutual connection across differences. Labor unions create mutual bonds along lines of class rather than those of race or religion. That is the fundamental reason why labor unions are such a target in fascist ideology.

There are more reasons why fascist ideology targets labor unions. Fascist politics is most effective under conditions of stark economic inequality. Research shows that a proliferation of labor unions is the best antidote to the development of such conditions. As the Harvard political scientist Archon Fung points out, "many societies that have low levels of inequality also have high participation in labor unions."[12] Fung notes an extraordinary statistic derived from a study of inequality and labor union density in OECD countries (most of the stable democracies in North America and Europe) in 2013. Fung points out that "countries with high union density have low income inequality (Denmark, Finland, Sweden, and Iceland), and the high inequality countries also have low union density (U.S., Chile, Mexico, and Turkey)." The number of countries in the study with high inequality and high union density was *zero*. Labor unions are a powerful weapon against the development of an unequal economic sphere. Because fascism thrives under conditions of economic uncertainty, where fear and resentment can be mobilized to set citizens against one another, labor unions guard against fascist politics' gaining a foothold.

In the United States, racial division has always countered the unifying force of the labor movement, which historically has threatened the owners of corporations, factories, and those with substantial investments in them. Chapter 14 of W.E.B. Du Bois's *Black Reconstruction* is en titled "Counter-Revolution of Property." In it, Du Bois describes the labor movement that emerged during Reconstruction as putting "such power in the hands of Southern labor that, with intelligent and unselfish leadership and a clarifying ideal, it could have rebuilt the economic foundations of Southern society, confiscated and redistributed wealth, and built a real democracy of industry for the masses of men."[13] Du Bois documents how the emerging Southern labor movement was riven by racial resentment, with poor whites fearful of losing their place in the social hierarchy above newly emancipated black citizens. Du Bois argues that Northern industrialists together with the old white Southern power structures employed these resentments to smash any semblance of a cross-racial labor movement, and with it what would have been a powerful force for economic equality. When poor white workers lack class identification with poor black workers, they fall back on familiar lines of racial division and resentment.

Today, "right to work" legislation has passed in twenty-eight U.S. states, and at the time of this writing threatens to be validated by the Supreme Court, at least for public labor unions. These laws forbid unions to collect dues from employees who do not wish to pay them, while requiring unions to provide employees who do not choose to pay dues equal union representation and rights. Such legislation is intended to destroy labor unions by removing their access to financial support. "Right to work" is an Orwellian name for legislation that attacks workers' ability to collectively bargain, thereby robbing workers of a voice. After right-to-work laws passed in the Midwestern bastions of American labor, Wisconsin and Michigan, the states' politics subsequently swung sharply right, especially during the racially divisive U.S. presidential campaign of 2016. It's worth investigating the history of right-to-work laws to understand their role in contemporary racial division.

Right-to-work laws began in the state of Texas in the 1940s, first proposed by a lobbyist named Vance Muse, in response to the fact that unions were challenging "the race-based political economy of the region." The Congress of Industrial Organizations (CIO) broke off from the American Federation of Labor (AFL) in the mid-1930s, due to the CIO's insistence on greater inclusivity, in particular the inclusion of unskilled labor. The CIO was, then, from its outset more progressive than the organization from which it broke off, and which it eventually rejoined to form today's AFL-CIO. As the Dartmouth sociologist Marc Dixon notes, CIO unions "tended to be more racially progressive than AFL unions . . . and often initiated campaigns to eliminate the poll tax in southern states during the early to mid-1940s."[14] Muse was the head of the Christian American Association, which had been a lobbying organization for oil firms. The Association was racist, anti-Semitic, and anti-Catholic, and it advanced its antiunion agenda with a familiar fascist program of fomenting panic about communists seeking racial equality to overthrow white domination.

Vance Muse was explicit about the racial motivation of the attack on unions via right-to-work laws: "From now on white women and white men will be forced into organizations with black African apes whom they will have to call 'brother' or lose their jobs." In 1945, Muse said, "They call me anti-Jew and anti-nigger. Listen, we like the nigger—in his place. . . . Our [right-to-work] amendment helps the nigger; it does not discriminate against him. Good niggers, not those Communist niggers. Jews? Why, some of my best friends are Jews. Good Jews." Muse declared himself "a southerner and for white supremacy," and the Christian Americans "considered the New Deal to be part of the broader assault of 'Jewish Marxism' upon Christian free enterprise."[15]

Right-to-work laws were originally advanced in language that mirrored precisely Hitler's attacks on trade unions in *Mein Kampf*. Nevertheless, their antiunion agenda, explicitly founded upon a desire to maintain white racial hierarchy and prevent solidarity across races and religions, has largely won the day in the United States today. Such antiunion policies paved the way for a presidential candidate running a white nationalist campaign with open nostalgia for the 1930s to sweep to victory across the once proud labor states of the Midwest.

. . .

Cracking down on unions and charging certain groups with laziness create the divisions that are crucial to the success of fascist politics. But why is *being lazy,* in fascist politics, constitutive of occupying the lower rungs in a hierarchy of social worth? And of all identities to glorify, why don't fascist politicians attempt to use, rather than disrupt, class unity? The answer lies in the social Darwinism at the basis of fascist politics.

Fascist movements share with social Darwinism the idea that life is a competition for power, according to which the division of society's resources should be left up to pure free market competition. Fascist movements share its ideals of hard work, private enterprise, and self-sufficiency. To have a life worthy of value, for the social Darwinist, is to have risen above others by struggle and merit, to have survived a fierce competition for resources. Those who do not compete successfully do not deserve the goods and resources of society. In an ideology that measures worth by productivity, propaganda that represents members of an out-group as lazy is a way to justify placing them lower on a hierarchy of worth.

This aspect of fascist ideology explains the National Socialist attitude toward the disabled, described as *lebensunwertes Leben*—life unworthy of life. Disabled citizens were regarded as lacking in value, because value in National Socialist ideology arose from the value of one's contributions to society through work. In Nazi ideology, those who depended on the state for their survival lacked value of any kind. Fascist governments have exhibited some of humanity's worst cruelty toward disabled populations. Nazi Germany's 1933 Law for the Prevention of Progeny with Hereditary Diseases mandated the sterilization of disabled citizens; this was subsequently followed by the secret T4 program, which carried out gassings of disabled German citizens, and eventually, in 1939, physicians were ordered to kill them.

We often think of fascism as anti-individualistic, deriving its power from uniform masses. Yet Hitler repeatedly extolled both the value of the individual and the ideal of meritocracy. It is the social Darwinist conception of individual worth that gives structure to fascist hierarchy and explains the charge of laziness. Groups are ordered, in fascism, by their capacity to achieve, to rise above others, in labor and war. Hitler decries liberal democracy because it embodies a contrary value system, one that grants worth independently of victory in a natural, meritocratic struggle. Hitler denounces democracy as *incompatible* with individuality, since it does not allow individual citizens to rise above others in competitive struggle. The fascist vision of individual freedom is similar to the libertarian notion of individual rights—the right to compete but not necessarily to succeed or even survive.

The doctrine of economic libertarianism understands freedom in a very specific way—freedom is defined by unconstrained free markets. It consists of having access to a "level playing field," in the form of markets that are not constrained in any way by regulations. If one ends up being weaker in the struggle, one's losses are one's own responsibility. Economic libertarianism connects both freedom and virtue with wealth. According to these principles, one "earns" one's freedom by accruing wealth in struggle. Those who do not "earn" their freedoms in this way do not deserve it. Though fascism involves a commitment to *group* hierarchies of worth that is flatly incompatible with true economic libertarianism, which does not generalize beyond the individual, both philosophies share a common principle by which value is measured. Economic libertarianism is, after all, the Manhattan dinner party face of social Darwinism.

In the 2012 American presidential election, vice presidential candidate Paul Ryan repeatedly spoke of American society being divided into "makers" and "takers." Ryan argued that it was imperative to advance policies that increase the number of "makers" in society and decrease the number of "takers." At the time, Ryan repeatedly raised the concern that the United States was becoming a society with a majority of "takers" and a minority of "makers," a society in which "takers" are those "who get more benefits in dollar value from the federal government than they pay back in taxes." According to this ideology, the "makers" in society, by virtue of their wealth, have more value than the "takers." More recently, Ryan has abandoned the vocabulary of "makers" versus "takers," but he has retained the same policies that clearly favor those with more wealth at the expense of those with less wealth. Those Americans inclined to place, for example, different skin colors on "makers" and "takers," in so doing, move beyond libertarianism into fascism.

Though libertarianism asserts individual freedom to compete in free markets, it also supports hierarchical companies. Fascist politics appreciates the libertarian philosophy for this reason, too. National Socialism recognized that workplaces were generally organized hierarchically, with an all-powerful CEO or plant leader. In the domain of private enterprise (as well as the military), National Socialism recognized a familiar authoritarian structure that its politics could propagandistically exploit. In the speeches of National Socialists, we find clear echoes of American right-wing politics, connecting government interference with loss of freedom and finding virtue in the leadership of a CEO.[16]

Hitler saw in private enterprise principles that aligned with his own ideology. The principle of meritocracy, by which "the great man" is rewarded for excellence by a position of leadership, appealed to him; the strong should rightly rule over the weak. Meritocracy, to Hitler, supported National Socialism's all-important leadership principle. Private workplaces are arranged hierarchically, with a command structure involving a CEO who issues orders (the fact that the CEO is answerable to a board of directors is a detail that is regularly ignored in fascist politics).

Hitler saw "two principles starkly opposed: the principle of democracy which, wherever its practical results are evident, is the principle of destruction. And the principle of the authority of the individual, which I would like to call the principle of achievement."[17] He warned that a democratic political sphere and an authoritarian economic sphere make for an unstable mix because the state has the tendency to encroach on business with democratically imposed regulations. Hitler emphasized that industrialists should support the Nazi movement, since business already operates according to "the leader principlc," the Führer Principle. In private enterprise, when a CEO gives the orders, the employees must comply; there is no room for democratic governance. Just so, in politics, Hitler urges, the leader should function like the CEO of a company.

Hitler had no appreciation for regulations that would protect either consumers or workers, just as he had no appreciation for the protections offered by welfare or labor unions. The basis of a commitment to a generous universal welfare system is an expression of the belief in the fundamental value of each citizen. The liberal democrat does not pit "makers" against "takers" in a competition for value. A generous social welfare system unites a community in mutual bonds of care, rather than dividing it into factions that demagogues can exploit. Labor unions bring together workers from different ethnic and religious backgrounds and across gender identity and sexual orientation in common goals—cooperating to bargain for a better deal.

All human institutions are flawed to some degree or other, social welfare systems and labor unions among them. But when critiquing the flaws of any institution, it is important to ask what would be lost in their absence. Jointly mobilizing for better conditions for everyone brings us together in ways that enable us to recognize a common humanity despite differences in appearance, ethnicity, religion, disability status, sexual orientation, and gender. Sadly, humans must continually be reminded that whether we are black or white, gender nonconforming or conforming, woman or man, Christian, Muslim, Jewish, Hindu, or atheist, we all need a weekend off, food to eat, and time and support to care for our aging parents. Flawed as the institutions and policies that give us our democratic ethos may be, a liberal democratic society without them risks collapse.

Hitler was not wrong that there are genuine tensions in a society that has a democratic political system and an economy based on private enterprises that function under principles of hierarchy. Many of us live in such societies, and hence live with the tensions bred in the conflict between democratic norms and economic ones. Out of such struggle, the labor movement has won the weekend, the eight-hour day, and many other victories, none of them trivial, but none ultimately democratically transformative. Hitler was correct that in a democratic society, there are tensions between the varied practices and structures of families, workplaces, government bodies, and civil society. Fascism promises to solve this by eliminating such differences. Instead, in fascist ideology, all institutions, from the family to the business to the state, would run according to the Führer Principle. The father, in fascist ideology, is the leader of the family; the CEO is the leader of the business; the authoritarian leader is the father, or the CEO, of the state. When voters in a democratic society yearn for a CEO as president, they are responding to their own implicit fascist impulses.

The pull of fascist politics is powerful. It simplifies human existence, gives us an object, a "them" whose supposed laziness highlights our own virtue and discipline, encourages us to identify with a forceful leader who helps us make sense of the world, whose bluntness regarding the "undeserving" people in the world is refreshing. If democracy looks like a successful business, if the CEO is tough-talking and cares little for democratic institutions, even denigrates them, so much the better. Fascist politics preys on the human frailty that makes our own suffering seem bearable if we know that those we look down upon are being made to suffer more.

Navigating the tensions created by living in a state with a democratic sphere of governance, a nondemocratic hierarchical economic sphere, and a rich, complex civil society replete with organizations, associations, and community groups adhering to multiple visions of a good life can be frustrating. Democratic citizenship requires a degree of empathy, insight, and kindness that demands a great deal of all of us. There are easier ways to live.

For example, we can reduce our public engagement to consumption, viewing our labor as whatever we need do to enter the consumer marketplace with money in our pockets, free to choose our widgets, to shape an identity based upon consumption.

Or we can go global and expand our understanding of "us" by wandering the world and appreciating its cultures and wonders, considering both the people living in the refugee camps of the world and the residents of small towns in Iowa to be our neighbors, while maintaining a connection with our own local traditions and duties.

But this engaging vision of the self moving through time and cultures is deeply problematic under conditions of stark economic inequality. It requires profound experiences with differences of all sorts. It may require an education that is generous, wise, committed to secular science and poetic truth. When in the United States it can take an entire family income to pay for a year at a good university for one child, we must ask, who of us ends up becoming members of such a successful and broad-minded citizenry? When universities are as expensive as they are in the United States, their generous liberal visions are easy targets for fascist demagoguery. Under conditions of stark economic inequality, when the benefits of liberal education, and the exposure to diverse cultures and norms, are available only to the wealthy few, liberal tolerance can be smoothly represented as elite privilege. Stark economic inequality creates conditions richly conducive to fascist demagoguery. It is fantasy to think that liberal democratic norms can flourish under such conditions.

EPILOGUE

The mechanisms of fascist politics all build on and support one another. They weave a myth of a distinction between "us" and "them," based in a romanticized fictional past featuring "us" and no "them," and supported by a resentment for a corrupt liberal elite, who take our hard-earned money and threaten our traditions. "They" are lazy criminals on whom freedom would be wasted (and who don't deserve it, in any case). "They" mask their destructive goals with the language of liberalism, or "social justice," and are out to destroy our culture and traditions and make "us" weak. "We" are industrious and law-abiding, having earned our freedoms through work; "they" are lazy, perverse, corrupt, and decadent. Fascist politics traffics in delusions that create these kinds of false distinctions between "us" and "them," regardless of obvious realities.

Some may complain about overreaction in the arguments I make, or object that the contemporary examples are not sufficiently extreme to juxtapose against the crimes of history. But the threat of the normalization of the fascist myth is real. It is tempting to think of "normal" as benign; when things are normal, there is no need for alarm. However, both history and psychology show that our *judgments* about normality can't always be trusted. In "Part Statistical, Part Evaluative," a 2017 paper in the journal *Cognition,* the Yale philosopher Joshua Knobe and his Yale psychology colleague Adam Bear demonstrate that judgments of normality are affected both by what people think is statistically normal and what they think is ideally normal, that is, healthy and proper (for example, hours per day of television watching).[1] In an article for the *New York Times* Sunday Review, they apply their conclusions to our judgments about the social world, finding that President Trump's continuing behavior—actions and speech that used to be considered remarkable—have real and disturbing consequences: "These actions are not simply coming to be regarded as more typical; they are coming to be seen as more normal. As a result, they will come to be seen as less bad and hence less worthy of outrage."[2]

Knobe and Bear's work provides a basis for a phenomenon that those who lived through transitions from democracy to fascism regularly emphasize from personal experience and with great alarm: the tendency of populations to normalize the once unthinkable. This is a central theme of my grandmother Ilse Stanley's 1957 memoir, *The Unforgotten*. My grandmother remained in Berlin until the last possible moment, in July 1939, so that she could continue working underground. From 1936 to Kristallnacht, she was venturing into the Sachsenhausen concentration camp, dressed as a Nazi social worker, rescuing from death hundreds of Jews confined there, one by one. In her book, she recounts the disparity between the extremes she witnessed in the concentration camp and the denials of the seriousness of the situation, its normalization, by the Jewish community of Berlin. She struggled to convince her neighbors of the truth:

> A concentration camp, for those on the outside, was a kind of labor camp. There were whispered rumors of people being beaten, even killed. But there was no comprehension of the tragic reality. We were still able to leave the country; we could still live in our homes; we could still worship in our temples; we were in a Ghetto, but the majority of our people were still alive.
>
> For the average Jew, this seemed enough. He didn't realize that we were all waiting for the end.
>
> The year was 1937.

In the United States, we have seen normalization of extreme policies with the rapid development of racialized mass incarceration, which occurred in my lifetime. More recently, in the United States, we have seen the normalization of mass shootings. In Hungary and Poland, which only recently were thriving liberal democracies, we have vivid examples of the rapid normalization of fascism. And we are now seeing the brutal public treatment of refugees and undocumented workers now normalized across the world. In the United States, as Donald Trump's campaign against immigration intensifies, it is sweeping untold numbers of undocumented workers of all backgrounds into anonymous privately run detention centers, where they are concealed from view and public concern.

What normalization does is transform the morally extraordinary into the ordinary. It makes us able to tolerate what was once intolerable by making it seem as if this is the way things have always been. By contrast, the word "fascist" has acquired a feeling of the extreme, like crying wolf. Normalization of fascist ideology, by definition, would make charges of "fascism" seem like an overreaction, even in societies whose norms are transforming along these worrisome lines. Normalization means precisely that encroaching ideologically extreme conditions are not recognized as such because they have come to seem normal. The charge of fascism will always seem extreme; normalization means that the goalposts for the legitimate use of "extreme" terminology continually move.

That our sense of the normal—and our ability to

judge it—is shifting does not mean that fascism is now upon us. What it means is that the intuitive sense that charges of "fascism" are exaggerated is not a good enough argument against the word's use. Rather, arguments about the encroachment of fascist politics need a specific understanding of its meaning and the tactics that fall under its umbrella.

Those who employ fascist tactics for political gain have varying goals. Now at least it does not appear that they seek to mobilize populations for world domination, as for example Hitler intended. Instead, though the goals are varied, there are common aspects of fascist thought and politics working in synergy. Since I am an American, I must note that one goal appears to be to use fascist tactics hypocritically, waving the banner of nationalism in front of middle- and working-class white people in order to funnel the state's spoils into the hands of oligarchs. At the same time, as during the Jim Crow era in the United States, politicians continue to assure their supporters that national identity, variously defined, provides status and dignity that are "priceless."

Fascist politics lures its audiences with the temptation of freedom from democratic norms while masking the fact that the alternative proposed is not a form of freedom that can sustain a stable nation state and can scarcely guarantee liberty. A state-based ethnic, religious, racial, or national conflict between "us" and "them" can hardly remain stable for long. And yes, even if fascism could sustain a stable state, would it be a good political community, a decent country within which children can be socialized to become empathetic human beings? Children can certainly be taught to hate, but to affirm hatred as a dimension of socialization has unintended consequences. Does anyone really want their children's sense of identity to be based on a legacy of marginalization of others?

Given the inevitability of increased climate change and its effects, the political and social instability of our times as discussed above, and the tension and conflicts inherent in growing global economic inequality, we will soon find ourselves confronted by movements of disadvantaged people across borders that dwarf those of previous eras, not excepting the movement of refugees in World War II. Traumatized, impoverished, and in need of aid, refugees, including legal immigrants, will be recast to fit racist stereotypes by leaders and movements committed to maintaining hierarchical group privilege and using fascist politics. Many thoughtful citizens throughout the world believe this process is already in play. Under a fascist agenda, the refugee narrative—life in refugee camps, the journey from fear and conflict to such camps, the hopelessness that accompanies extended time in these places—rather than engendering empathy, is cast as the origin story of terrorism and danger. These populations struggle through unspeakable horrors to reach safer shores. That even such people could be painted as fundamental threats is a testament to the illusory power of fascist myth. I have tried, in the pages of this book, to spell out its structure so that it can be recognized and resisted.

The challenges we will face are enormous. How do we maintain a sense of common humanity, when fear and insecurity will lead us to flee into the comforting arms of mythic superiority in vain pursuit of a sense of dignity? Vexing questions define our times. Nonetheless, we can take comfort in the histories of progressive social movements, which against long odds and hard struggle have in the past succeeded in the project of eliciting empathy.

In the direct targets of fascist politics—refugees, feminism, labor unions, racial, religious, and sexual minorities—we can see the methods used to divide us. But we must never forget that the chief target of fascist politics is its intended audience, those it seeks to ensnare in its illusory grip, to enroll in a state where everyone deemed "worthy" of human status is increasingly subjugated by mass delusion. Those not included in that audience and status wait in the camps of the world, straw men and women ready to be cast into the roles of rapists, murderers, terrorists. By refusing to be bewitched by fascist myths, we remain free to engage one another, all of us flawed, all of us partial in our thinking, experience, and understanding, but none of us demons.

ACKNOWLEDGMENTS

My mother, Sara Stanley, and father, Manfred Stanley, are refugees to the United States, both having lived through the horrors of anti-Semitism in Western and Eastern Europe. My father lived through Kristallnacht, ten days before his sixth birthday. My mother is from Eastern Poland, and survived in a Siberian labor camp before being repatriated back to Warsaw in 1945, where she and her parents experienced the brutality of Polish postwar anti-Semitism. I was raised also with the legacy of my grandmother, Ilse Stanley, whose memoir of the 1930s in Berlin, *The Unforgotten,* informs these pages. My family background has saddled me with difficult emotional baggage. But it also, crucially, prepared me to write this book.

But this book is not, of course, rooted just in Europe. One of my central intellectual influences is my stepmother, Mary Stanley. Mary came into my life early and helped root me in American history. Thanks to her, I learned early on in life about abolitionism, the history of the labor movement, and, above all, the civil rights movement, in which she participated as a college student. It's not much of an exaggeration to say that my mother's and father's outlooks are pessimistic—an emotional legacy I grapple with as I try not to pass it on to yet another generation. Mary has always been there to remind me to leave 10 percent for hope; her voice echoes through the pages of this book in just such moments. She also carefully read multiple drafts, and certain sections are essentially the results of her comments. I am so fortunate to have her in my life, and I owe her a great debt of gratitude.

Mary's was not the only voice who helped me see the centrality of U.S. history to fascism. I have been generously blessed with close friends, such as the U.S. historian Donna Murch and the philosopher Kristie Dotson, who patiently talked with me about the ways in which U.S. racism affected the rise of European fascism. Dotson and Murch were only part of a generous research team, whose New Haven branch was headed by Timothy Snyder and Marci Shore, and contained as members Reginald Dwayne Betts, Robin Dembroff, Zoltan Gendler-Szabo, Antuan Johnson, Ben Justice, Titus Kaphar, Kathryn Lofton, Tracey Meares, Claudia Rankine, Jennifer Richeson, and Anshul Verma (this is, regrettably, only a partial list). I am grateful to my group of friends in New Haven for their generous engagement with my work. I also must acknowledge a debt of gratitude to the undergraduate students who have taken my Propaganda, Ideology, and Democracy course, and from whom I have learned so much over the years. Outside of New Haven, a number of thinkers have affected my thinking about the topics in this book, including Lewis Gordon, Lori Gruen, Howard Kahn, Sari Kisilevsky, Michael Lynch, Kate Manne, Charles Mills, David Livingstone Smith, Amia Srinivasan, Ken Taylor, Lynne Tirrell, Elizabeth Anderson, and Peter Railton. Thanks to Brian Leiter and Samuel Leiter for challenging me to explain how the theory of propaganda in my 2015 book was relevant to fascist policies.[1] I owe a particularly large debt to the linguist David Beaver, who is the coauthor of another book I am working on, for Princeton University Press, called *Hustle: The Politics of Language.* David has been an invaluable interlocutor throughout this process.

This book originated with a suggestion from my Princeton University Press editor, Rob Tempio, to follow up my 2015 book, *How Propaganda Works,* with a work on fascism. I am grateful for his intellectual generosity and confidence in my capacities to do politically important work. I had never before written a trade book. On the recommendation of friends, I reached out to agents and decided to employ Stephanie Steiker, of Regal Hoffman & Associates, as my agent. When we began our working relationship in the summer of 2017, I had a two-page sketch of this book. In early September, we met for the first time. Stephanie constantly supported me, told me the unvarnished truth when I needed to hear it, and (equally important) concealed it from me when it would be too damaging. She read countless very early versions, and multiple times steered me away from shoals and into open water. An equal amount of immense good fortune came in the form of my Random House editor, Molly Turpin. After acquiring the rights to the book in November 2017, she read a good half-dozen drafts, supplying me with essentially line by line edits. Insofar as the writing in this book stands out, a large amount of the credit goes to her. I am deeply indebted to both Stephanie and Molly.

At home in New Haven, my mother-in-law, Karen Ambush Thande, has continually been a source of support in multiple ways, for example, serving as a crucial sounding board for ideas, using her deep knowledge of the Black American tradition upon which I here draw. My children, Alain and Emile, are my source of greatest joy, as well as living reminders of the necessity of this work. I have been struggling hard to pass on the wisdom that comes from their legacies, while avoiding saddling them with their psychic burdens. If I achieve that, it will be my greatest victory. Finally, as ever, my greatest debt is to my partner, Njeri Thande. There is no one to whom I am more indebted, and also no one I hold in higher esteem.

NOTES

Introduction

1. Charles Lindbergh, "Aviation, Geography, and Race," *Reader's Digest,* Nov. 1939, 64–67.
2. See Richard Steigmann-Gall, "Star-spangled Fascism: American Interwar Political Extremism in Comparative Perspective," *Social History* 42:1 (2017): 94–119.
3. See Nour Kteily and Emile Bruneau, "Backlash: The Politics and Real-World Consequences of Minority Group Dehumanization," *Personality and Social Psychology Bulletin* 43:1 (2017): 87–104.

Chapter 1: The Mythic Past

1. "Fascism's Myth: The Nation," in Roger Griffin, ed., *Fascism* (Oxford: Oxford University Press, 1995), 43–44.
2. Alfred Rosenberg, "The Folkish Idea of State," in *Nazi Ideology Before 1933: A Documentation,* ed. Barbara Miller Lane and Leila J. Rupp (Austin: University of Texas Press, 1978), 60–74, 67.
3. "Motherhood and Warriorhood as the Key to National Socialism," in Griffin, *Fascism,* 123.
4. "The New German Woman," in Griffin, *Fascism,* 137.
5. Richard Grunberger, *The 12-Year Reich: A Social History of Nazi Germany 1933–45* (New York: Da Capo Press, 1971), 252–53.
6. Charu Gupta, "Politics of Gender: Women in Nazi Germany," *Economic and Political Weekly* 26:17 (April 1991).

7. weev, "Just What Are Traditonal Gender Roles?" *The Daily Stormer,* May 2017. https.//dailystormer.name/just-what-are-traditional-gender-roles/.
8. Bernard Mees, *The Science of the Swastika* (Budapest: Central European University Press, 2008), 115.
9. Hannah Beech, "'There Is No Such Thing as Rohingya': Myanmar Erases a History," *New York Times,* December 2, 2017.
10. https://www.tagesspiegel.de/politik/hoecke-rede-im-wortlaut-gemuetszustand-eines-total-besiegten-volkes/19273518.html.
11. H. Himmler, "Zum Gleit," Germanien 8 (1936): 193, after Bernard Mees, *The Science of the Swastika* (Budapest, Central European University Press, 2008), 124.
12. Katie N. Rotella and Jennifer A. Richeson, "Motivated to 'Forget': The Effects of In-Group Wrongdoing on Memory and Collective Guilt," *Social Psychological and Personality Science* 4:6 (2013): 730–37.
13. B. Sahdra and M. Ross, "Group Identification and Historical Memory," *Personality and Social Psychology Bulletin* 33 (2017): 384–95.
14. See, e.g., Ishaan Tharoor, "Hungary's Orbán Invokes Ottoman Invasion to Justify Keeping Refugees Out," *Washington Post,* September 4, 2015.

Chapter 2: Propaganda

1. Elizabeth Hinton, *From the War on Poverty to the War on Crime: The Making of Mass Incarceration in America* (Cambridge, MA: Harvard University Press, 2016), 142.
2. Richard Grunberger, *The 12-Year Reich: A Social History of Nazi Germany 1933–1945* (New York: Da Capo Press, 1995), 90.
3. W.E.B. Du Bois, *Black Reconstruction,* (New York: Oxford University Press, 2014), 419.
4. Ibid., 583.
5. Kate Manne, in *Down Girl: The Logic of Misogyny* (New York: Oxford University Press, 2018), has argued that a similar dialectic was in play in Clinton's 2016 loss to Trump (see 256–63 and 271).
6. Peter Pomerantsev, *Nothing Is True and Everything Is Possible: The Surreal Heart of the New Russia* (New York: PublicAffairs, 2014), 65.
7. See Ozan O. Varol, "Stealth Authoritarianism," *Iowa Law Review,* vol. 100 (2015): 1673–1742, 1677.
8. Frederick Douglass, "What to the Slave Is the Fourth of July?," July

5, 1852. Available at https://www.thenation.com/article/what-slave-fourth-july-frederick-douglass.

9. Ibid.
10. Bernard Mees, *The Science of the Swastika* (Budapest: Central European University Press, 2008), 112–13.
11. https://www.youtube.com/watch?v=TTZJoCWuhXE.

Chapter 3: Anti-intellectual

1. For example, Chris Caesar describes the strategy of Trump's campaign this way in "Trump Ran Against Political Correctness. Now His Team Is Begging for Politeness," *Washington Post,* May 16, 2017.
2. Robert O'Harrow Jr. and Shawn Boburg, "How a 'Shadow' Universe of Charities Joined with Political Warriors to Fuel Trump's Rise," *Washington Post,* June 3, 2017.
3. Fernanda Zamudio-Suarez, "Missouri Lawmaker Who Wants to Eliminate Tenure Says It's 'Un-American,'" *Chronicle of Higher Education,* January 12, 2017.
4. Charu Gupta, "Politics of Gender: Women in Nazi Germany," *Economic and Political Weekly* 26:17 (1991): 40–48.
5. Masha Gessen, *The Future Is History: How Totalitarianism Reclaimed Russia* (New York: Riverhead Books, 2017). Quotes are from 264–67.
6. Fred Weir, "Why Is Someone Trying to Shutter One of Russia's Top Private Universities?" *Christian Science Monitor,* March 28, 2017.
7. See Jedidiah Purdy's excellent *New Yorker* article from March 19, 2015, "Ayn Rand Comes to UNC," from which I obtained the information about North Carolina in the previous two paragraphs.
8. See Annie Linskey, "With Patience, and a Lot of Money, Kochs Sow Conservatism on Campuses," *Boston Globe,* February 2, 2018.
9. "In Turkey, Crackdown on Academics Heats Up," Voice of America, February 14, 2017.
10. Cited in "Science Scorned" (editorial), *Nature* 467.133, September 2010.
11. Pierre Drieu la Rochelle, "The Rebirth of European Man," in Roger Griffin, ed., *Fascism,* (Oxford: Oxford University Press, 2010), 202–203.
12. Adolf Hitler, *Mein Kampf* (*My Battle*) (Boston and New York: Houghton Mifflin Company, The Riverside Press Cambridge, 1933, Abridged and Translated by E. T. S. Dugdale, 76–77.

13. Victor Klemperer, *The Language of the Third Reich* (New York: Continuum, 1947), 20–21.
14. "Fascist Mysticism," in Griffin, *Fascism,* 55.
15. Michael Lewis, "Has Anyone Seen the President?" *Bloomberg View,* February 9, 2018.

Chapter 4: Unreality

1. Hannah Arendt, *The Origins of Totalitarianism* (New York: Harcourt, Brace, 1973), 351.
2. Ernst Cassirer, "The Technique of the Modern Political Myths," chapter 18 of *The Myth of the State* (New Haven: Yale University Press, 1946).
3. See Brian Tashman's October 30, 2014, article "Tony Perkins: Gay Rights Part of Population Control Agenda" in *Right Wing Watch.*
4. See Oliver Hahl, Minjae Kim, and Ezra Zuckerman, "The Authentic Appeal of the Lying Demagogue," *American Sociological Review,* February 2018.
5. https://www.thenation.com/article/exclusive-lee-atwaters-infamous-1981-interview-southern-strategy/.

Chapter 5: Hierarchy

1. See Jim Sidanius and Felicia Pratto, *Social Dominance: An Intergroup Theory of Social Hierarchy and Oppression* (New York: Cambridge University Press, 1999).
2. Felicia Pratto, Jim Sidanius, and Shana Levin, "Social Dominance Theory and the Dynamics of Intergroup Relations: Taking Stock and Looking Forward," *European Review of Social Psychology* 17:1, 271–320, at 271–72.
3. http://teachingamericanhistory.org/library/document/cornerstone-speech/.
4. W.E.B. Du Bois, "Of the Ruling of Men," in W.E.B. Du Bois, *Darkwater* (Dover, 1999).
5. Alfred Rosenberg, "The Protocols of the Elders of Zion and Jewish World Policy," 44–59 of *Nazi Ideology Before 1933: A Documentation,* ed. Barbara Miller Lane and Leila J. Rupp (Austin: University of Texas Press, 1978), 55.

Chapter 6: Victimhood

1. W.E.B. Du Bois, *Black Reconstruction in America: 1860–80* (New York: Free Press, 1935), 283.
2. Michael Kraus, Julian Rucker, and Jennifer Richeson, "Americans Misperceive Racial Economic Equality," *Proceedings of the National Academy of Sciences of the United States of America* 114:39, 10324–31.
3. A classic early paper is Herbert Blumer's "Race Prejudice as a Sense of Group Position," *Pacific Sociological Review* 1:1 (Spring 1958): 3–7.
4. Maureen Craig and Jennifer Richeson, "On the Precipice of a 'Majority-Minority' America: Perceived Status Threat from the Racial Demographic Shift Affects White Americans' Political Ideology," *Psychological Science* 25:6 (2014): 1189–97.
5. M. A. Craig, J. M. Rucker, and J. A. Richeson, "Racial and Political Dynamics of an Approaching 'Majority-Minority' United States," *Annals of the American Academy of Political and Social Science* (in press, April 2018).
6. Michael Kimmel, *Angry White Men: American Masculinity at the End of an Era* (New York: Nation Books, 2013), 110–11.
7. Ibid., 112.
8. See Kate Manne, *Down Girl: The Logic of Misogyny* (New York: Oxford Press, 2018), 156–57.

Chapter 7: Law and Order

1. Shanette C. Porter, Michelle Rheinschmidt-Same, and Jennifer Richeson, "Inferring Identity from Language: Linguistic Intergroup Bias Informs Social Categorization," *Psychological Science* 27:1 (2016): 94–102.
2. James Baldwin, "Negroes Are Anti-Semitic Because They Are Anti-White," *New York Times,* April 9, 1967.
3. Nic Subtirelu, "Covering Baltimore: Protest or Riot?" *Linguistic Pulse: Analyzing the Circulation of Discourse in Society,* April 29, 2015.
4. David Roodman, "The Impacts of Incarceration on Crime Open Philanthropy Project," September 2017.
5. See Amy Lerman and Vesla Weaver, *The Democratic Consequences of American Crime Control* (Chicago: University of Chicago Press, 2014).
6. W. E. Burghardt Du Bois, *The Annals of the American Academy of Political and Social Science,* 11:1–23, January 1898.

7. Aneeta Rattan, Cynthia Levine, Carol Dweck, and Jennifer Eberhardt, "Race and the Fragility of the Legal Distinction Between Juveniles and Adults," *PLoS ONE* 7:5, May 23, 2012.
8. Rebecca C. Hetey and Jennifer L. Eberhardt, "Racial Disparities in Incarceration Increase Acceptance of Punitive Policies," *Psychological Science* 25:10 (2014): 1949–54.

Chapter 8: Sexual Anxiety

1. Keith Nelson, "The 'Black Horror on the Rhine': Race as a Factor in Post–World War I Diplomacy," *Journal of Modern History* 42.4 (December 1970): 606–27.
2. "Rape, Racism, and the Myth of the Black Rapist," in Angela Davis, *Women, Race and Class* (New York: Random House, 1981), 173.
3. Crystal Nicole Feimster, *Southern Horrors: Women and the Politics of Rape and Lynching* (Cambridge, MA: Harvard University Press, 2009), 78–79.
4. See, e.g., Ibid., 90.
5. Charu Gupta, "The Myth of Love Jihad," *Indian Express,* August 28, 2014. Gupta also has an academic article on the Love Jihad myth, "Allegories of 'Love Jihad' and Ghar Vāpasī: Interlocking the Socio-Religious with the Political," *Archiv Orientální* 84 (2016): 291–316.
6. Julia Serano, *Whipping Girl: A Transsexual Woman on Sexism and the Scapegoating of Femininity* (Berkeley: Seal Press, 2007), 15.
7. Johanna Laakso, "Friends and Foes of 'Freedom,'" *Hungarian Spectrum* (online), December 28, 2017.

Chapter 9: Sodom and Gomorrah

1. *Mein Kampf,* 52.
2. Adolf Hitler, Gerhard Weinberg, and Krista Smith, *Hitler's Second Book: The Unpublished Sequel to Mein Kampf* (Enigma Books, 2006), 26.
3. Alfred Rosenberg, "German Freedom as a Prerequisite for Folk Culture," in *Nazi Ideology Before 1933: A Documentation,* ed. Barbara Miller Lane and Leila J. Rupp (Austin: University of Texas Press, 1978), 124–26.
4. "Official Party Statement on Its Attitude Toward the Farmers and Agriculture," in Lane and Rupp, *Nazi Ideology Before 1933,* 118–23.
5. Ibid., 122.

6. Maria Sacchetti and Emily Guskin, "In Rural America, Fewer Immigrants and Less Tolerance," *Washington Post,* June 17, 2017.
7. Lucy Pasha-Robinson, "French Election: Marine Le Pen Wins Just 5% of Paris Vote While FN Rural Support Surges," *Independent,* April 24, 2017.
8. https://www.bbc.com/news/world-europe-39870460.
9. Nico Passchier, "The Electoral Geography of the Nazi Landslide: The Need for Community Studies," in *Who Were the Fascists,* ed. Stein Ugelvik Larsen, Bernt Hagtvet, and Jan Petter Myklebust (Oslo: Universitatsforlaget, 1980), 283–300.
10. Elliot Ackerman, "Atatürk Versus Erdoğan: Turkey's Long Struggle," *New Yorker,* July 16, 2016.
11. From the chapter "The Jews" in Richard Grunberger, *The 12-Year Reich: A Social History of Nazi Germany 1933–1945* (New York: Da Capo Press, 1995), 458.
12. *Mein Kampf,* 9.
13. R. W. Darré, "The Peasantry as the Key to Understanding the Nordic Race," in Lane and Rupp, *Nazi Ideology Before 1933,* 103–106.
14. See Masha Gessen, *The Future Is History: How Totalitarianism Reclaimed Russia* (New York: Riverhead Books, 2017), 374–75, for Putin's obsession with birthrates.
15. Benito Mussolini, "The Strength in Numbers," in Roger Griffin, ed., *Fascism* (Oxford: Oxford University Press), 58–59.
16. *Mein Kampf,* 127.
17. Gregory Paul Wegner, *Anti-Semitism and Schooling Under the Third Reich* (New York: Routledge / Studies in the History of Education, 2002), 59.

Chapter 10: Arbeit Macht Frei

1. "Guidelines of the German Workers' Party," *Nazi Ideology Before 1933: A Documentation,* ed., Barbara Miller Lane and Leila J. Rupp (Austin: University of Texas Press, 1978), 10.
2. Martin Gilens, "'Race Coding' and White Opposition to Welfare," *American Political Science Review* 90.3 (September 1996): 593–604.
3. Hannah Arendt, "The Seeds of a Fascist International," *Jewish Frontier* 1945, 12–16. Passage appears on p. 147 of Hannah Arendt, *Essays in Understanding,* ed. Jerome Kohn (New York: Random House, 1994).
4. Timothy Snyder, *Black Earth: The Holocaust as History and Warning* (New York: Crown, 2015), 228.

5. "Situation of Human Rights of Rohingya Muslims and Other Minorities in Myanmar," Report of the United Nations High Commissioner for Human Rights, Annual Report of the United Nations High Commissioner for Human Rights and Reports of the High Commissioner and the Secretary-General, June 28, 2016.
6. Frantz Fanon, *Black Skin, White Masks* (New York, Grove Press, 2008), 73.
7. Devah Pager, "The Mark of a Criminal Record," *American Journal of Sociology* 108:5 (March 2003): 937–75.
8. Douglas Blackmon, *Slavery by Another Name: The Reenslavement of Black Americans from the Civil War to World War II* (New York: Doubleday, 2008).
9. Elizabeth Hinton, *From the War on Poverty to the War on Crime: The Making of Mass Incarceration in America,* (Cambridge, MA: Harvard University Press, 2016),163.
10. Lewis Gordon, *Bad Faith and Anti-Black Racism* (Humanity Books, 1995). See also Charles Mills, "White Ignorance," in Shannon Sullivan and Nancy Tuana, *Race and Epistemologies of Ignorance* (SUNY Press, 2007), 13–38, and Gaile Pohlhaus, "Relational Knowing and Epistemic Injustice: Toward a Theory of Willful Hermeneutical Ignorance," *Hypatia: A Journal of Feminist Philosophy* 27:4 (2012): 715–35.
11. *Mein Kampf,* 258.
12. Archon Fung, "It's the Gap, Stupid," *Boston Review,* September 1, 2017.
13. W.E.B. Du Bois, *Black Reconstruction in America: 1860–1880* (New York: Free Press, 1935), 580.
14. Marc Dixon, "Limiting Labor: Business Political Mobilization and Union Setback," *States Journal of Policy History* 19.2 (2007): 313–44.
15. Michael Pierce, "The Origins of Right to Work: Vance Muse, Anti-Semitism, and the Maintenance of Jim Crow Labor Relations," *Labor and Working Class History Organization,* January 12, 2017.
16. For more on the anti-liberal consequences of economic libertarianism and the themes in these paragraphs, see Elizabeth Anderson's 2017 book *Private Government: How Employers Rule Our Lives (And Why We Don't Talk About It),* (Princeton University Press, 2017).
17. Hitler's Speech to the Industry Club in Düsseldorf, in Max Domarus, ed., *Hitler: Speeches and Proclamations 1932–1945, The Chronicle of a Dictatorship* (London: I. B. Tauris, 1990), vol. 1, 94–95.

Epilogue

1. Adam Bear and Joshua Knobe, "Normality: Part Statistical, Part Evaluative," *Cognition,* vol. 167 (October 2017): 25–37.
2. Adam Bear and Joshua Knobe, "The Normalization Trap," *New York Times* Sunday Review, January 28, 2017.

Acknowledgments

1. Brian Leiter and Samuel Leiter, "Not Your Grandfather's Propaganda," *The New Rambler Review,* October 2015.

INDEX

PHOTO: © EDWIN TSE

JASON STANLEY is the Jacob Urowsky Professor of Philosophy at Yale University. He is the author of *Know How*; *Languages in Context*; *Knowledge and Practical Interests,* which won the 2007 American Philosophical Association book prize; and *How Propaganda Works,* which won the 2016 PROSE Award for Philosophy from the Association of American Publishers. He is a frequent contributor to *The New York Times, The Washington Post, Boston Review,* and *The Chronicle of Higher Education,* among other publications. Stanley lives in New Haven, Connecticut, with his family.

jason-stanley.com

Twitter: @jasonintrator